The Patented Works of J. Hutton Pulitzer

INPUT DEVICE FOR ALLOWING INTERFACE TO A WEB SITE IN ASSOCIATION WITH A UNIQUE INPUT CODE

Patent Number: 8,069,098
Date of Patent: November 29, 2011

A Contradiction in Time

In 1985, leaving the comfortable world of a Fortune 500 company to pursue my own entrepreneurial dreams/venture was a mutually terrifying and electrifying proposition.

At that time, comfort for me was defined as "Corporate America". And my mega-corporation world included over twenty-five years spent in Senior Executive positions with AT&T, General Electric, Oracle and British Telecom.

But in 1985 I took that "leap of faith" and purchased a company whereby I could pursue my entrepreneurial dreams. In doing so, I inherited a young employee associated with that company who I immediately recognized had great potential. He was smart, quick to learn and searching for knowledge to become a powerful and influential force in both the business world and society (his career had just begun). He left an indelible impression on me, one that has been branded in my mind for over thirty years (as I write this prologue).

This initial venture in 1985 was my first into the mostly solo activities associated with the entrepreneurial world. In the 80's becoming an Entrepreneur was the "New-New". Most seasoned executives in Corporate America wanted to become one, and all had taken full notice of the ultimate entrepreneur – STEVE JOBS – as the dynamic entrepreneur who could build a huge company, and yet still move and be as nimble as a newly minted entrepreneur.

During this time, all seasoned executives were "*In Search of Excellence*" (by Tom Peters). Dreams were big and visionaries were leading the way; but few either had the nerve or possessed the willing to take the risk outside of the corporate world to be a true entrepreneur.

With that first acquisition of a small company came one individual, which would change my life in many ways. Funny, to even type that since I was the seasoned Fortune 500 Executive who was going to teach him the ways of the corporate world and this person was just barely out of his teens.

From the day, as the new company owner and meeting him, my soul knew he would accomplish great things. Great things, maybe not in the traditional orthodox manner that most people understand/expect, but in a manner that is unique to HIS way of achieving his goals for mankind. I trusted my natural instincts then and he has proven them right to this day.

Just as with any business, time marches on and things change and within a few years this young visionary left my tutelage to forge his own entrepreneurial path. Coming from the mega corporation's culture and now eighteen years as an

entrepreneur, I have had the opportunity to work with extremely talented individuals, but none can match the creative mind/talents of J. Hutton Pulitzer.

Pulitzer is the ultimate contradiction if they're ever was one. The duality of what he was and could be is amazing. On one hand an incredible presenter and salesman, while on the other a loner/society recluse. An incredible technical genius that does not write a lick of code, a maniacal visionary who often runs and thinks too fast for the average person, but yet continually alters his activities to help others to understand and/or succeed; but yet probably cares too much about what people think at times.

Truly a contradiction:

Like Steve Jobs, Pulitzer's mind thinks and works differently when it comes to life and impacting society in multiple ways. One of his most cherished achievements was the development and implementation of the world's first "global positioning system for the Internet" (i.e. the CueCat™). Definitely ahead of the times, Pulitzer's vision for accessing the Internet in a unique manner was sponsored and financed by such corporate giants as RadioShack, ING Barings, Coca-Cola, NBC, etc. for a total of $200 million and successful individuals such as Steven Spielberg, Steve Forbes, etc. Top manufacturers and corporations throughout the world understood and invested in the :CRQ Cue Code technology because they shared Pulitzer's vision and knew it would "bridge the gap" between consumers and their companies. But consumers were slow to "understand" the new technology and the Internet market crash in 2000-2001 ended the rapid success of his company's (Digital Convergence, Inc.) technology in its initial form; but yet still today, over two billion consumers around the world a day utilize some derivative of his initial patents.

Nevertheless, Pulitzer's patents and his creative visions continue to thrive in today's highly complex and technological environment. Even today, when you board an American Airlines flight, the boarding agent utilizes a derivative of Pulitzer's scanning patent when he/she scans your Boarding Pass for the flight. And Smart Phones of all types/manufacturers utilize the patented technology that Pulitzer originally invented with his Chief Technology Officer at Digital Convergence in the late 1990's.

Bottom line, society should not dismiss or misjudge Pulitzer in the future. Other entrepreneurs like him who themselves have failed several times in their careers have proven to be geniuses when their total careers are evaluated. Pulitzer is the ultimate Type "A" personality and he continues to think creatively and decisively, which in time will certainly impact our lives again...... I can guarantee this!

To this day, more than 30 years later, we still work together. It is certainly a challenge to work beside him but I feel honored to be his co-worker and friend. Today our roles have changed and I am learning from him. To understand him is

to learn to love him and his personification of a contradiction. Fact is he does not let many inside personally; whether its too painful or he is just too driven and focused, remains to be seen. But you have to respect his accomplishments and recognize that there is more than one way to accomplish greatness.

That's my personal dialog about Hutton, but if I were talking to a business executive who was inquiring about Hutton and wanting to know "if the myths about him are true" I would answer in the following manner:

As a trusted and extraordinary individual, J. Hutton Pulitzer has continually demonstrated a unique ability to see ahead in time and forecast the future with an uncanny degree of accuracy. Many times over the past 32 years that I have known him, he has creatively and successfully leveraged his visions of the future in order to insure the success of many types of business ventures.

Having experienced the agony of competitive inroads associated with some of his early projects, Hutton quickly studied all aspects surrounding the sophisticated art of drafting patents and has "mastered" the ability to author and construct patents in a manner that are "iron clad" in blocking competitive inroads by outside entities. His effectiveness can be substantiated via his present patent portfolio, which includes global patents granted in 189 countries (a feat most inventors never attain).

His unique and personal approach in constructing patents has proven to be extremely successful which is further substantiated by his single best unmatched patent ratio of forty-nine citations per one patent (i.e. 49:1 ratio) and the fact that he currently holds an unparalleled patent granted record of 98.8%.

In addition to authoring unique and complex patents, he is extremely experienced in the art of constructing original patents in such a manner as to anticipate future potential infringements associated with any/all patents he writes. Hutton takes a multi-dimensional view of possible competitive inroads, as well as, the anticipation of the creative and unique ways in which his patents can be implemented. Thereby, re-enforcing the protection armor in which he builds into each and every patent he develops.

Bottom-line, his patent expertise routinely exceeds his client's and/or the industry's expectations; while effectively insuring each and every patent he develops in such a manner as to prevent any potential work around and/or patent penetration in future years. As a result, patent experts from around the world routinely keep a keen eye on Mr. Pulitzer's patent work and filings in order to possibly anticipate his vision and actions regarding the future.

As the result of Pulitzer's developing an industry around connecting codes where one did not exist before, he became the "Father" of what is now known as "Scan-To-Connect" and "Scan Commerce". Two brand new features Hutton bestowed upon the Internet in the late 90's.

But with every new industry and technology comes competition and jealously; therefore I will quote one Billionaire's comment about Pulitzer's idea for bar codes to connect to the Internet via scanning:

"The stupidest invention ever!"

That quote, which was carried by numerous newspapers, magazines and blogs when uttered was like the shot heard around the world at the time the dot com industry was crashing in 2000-2001.

But like Steve Jobs, Pulitzer is a patient man and visionaries do NOT let their dreams die. Pulitzer implemented his vision and pursued his patents for "Scan to Commerce" and "Scan to Connect" and as I mentioned above, today over two billion people around the world utilize a derivative of his original scanning patents on a daily basis. ***A multibillion-dollar industry created from the vision of a "contradiction in time".***

I say, in closing *"Two Billion daily users of his technology a day! Not bad for the stupidest invention ever!"*

Can't wait to see his next stupid idea!

Blaine L. Thacker, Ex-Corporate Executive & Entrepreneur

P.S. You should view the movie "JOBS" (i.e. Steve Jobs) to truly understand and appreciate J. Hutton Pulitzer.

(12) **United States Patent**
Philyaw et al.

(10) Patent No.: **US 8,069,098 B2**
(45) **Date of Patent:** **Nov. 29, 2011**

(54) **INPUT DEVICE FOR ALLOWING INTERFACE TO A WEB SITE IN ASSOCIATION WITH A UNIQUE INPUT CODE**

(75) Inventors: **Jeffry Jovan Philyaw**, Dallas, TX (US); **David Kent Mathews**, Carrollton, TX (US)

(73) Assignee: **RPX-LV Acquisition LLC**, Wilmington, DE (US)

(*) Notice: Subject to any disclaimer, the term of this patent is extended or adjusted under 35 U.S.C. 154(b) by 618 days.

(21) Appl. No.: **12/235,456**

(22) Filed: **Sep. 22, 2008**

(65) **Prior Publication Data**

US 2009/0106450 A1   Apr. 23, 2009

Related U.S. Application Data

(63) Continuation of application No. 09/494,924, filed on Feb. 1, 2000, now Pat. No. 7,428,499, which is a continuation of application No. 09/378,221, filed on Aug. 19, 1999, now Pat. No. 6,745,234, which is a continuation-in-part of application No. 09/151,471, filed on Sep. 11, 1998, now abandoned, and a continuation-in-part of application No. 09/151,530, filed on Sep. 11, 1998, now Pat. No. 6,098,106.

(51) **Int. Cl.**
G06Q 10/00   (2006.01)
(52) **U.S. Cl.** **705/28**; 705/22; 705/23
(58) **Field of Classification Search** .... None
See application file for complete search history.

(56) **References Cited**

U.S. PATENT DOCUMENTS

3,668,312 A   6/1972   Yamamoto et al.
(Continued)

FOREIGN PATENT DOCUMENTS

CA   2250450   4/1999
(Continued)

OTHER PUBLICATIONS

"Bar Code Method for Automating Catalog Orders," IBM Technical Disclosure Bulletin, No. 88A 61554, Sep. 1988, pp. 243-244.
Bragg, Steven M., Accounting Best Practices, John Wiley and Sons, Inc., 1999.
Curtis, S.P.; "Transponder technologies, applications and benefits" Use of Electronic Transponders in Automation, IEEE Colloquium on, Feb. 15, 1989 pp. 2/1-218.
Defler, Frank J. et. al. How Networks Work, Millennium Ed., Que Corporation, Nov. 2000.

(Continued)

Primary Examiner — F. Zeender
Assistant Examiner — Christopher Buchanan
(74) *Attorney, Agent, or Firm* — Howison & Arnott, L.L.P.

(57)   **ABSTRACT**

An input device for allowing interface to a web site in association with a unique input code. A method for interconnecting a first location on a global communication network with a second location thereon is disclosed. An input device is provided at the first location on the global communication network having associated therewith a unique input device ID. A product code disposed on a product is scanned with the input device, which product code is representative of the product in commercial transactions, the operation of scanning operable to extract the information contained in the product code to provide a unique value as an output. The unique value is then associated with the unique input device ID. In response to the operation of scanning and associating, the first location is connected to the second location.

20 Claims, 10 Drawing Sheets

U.S. PATENT DOCUMENTS

3,886,328 A	5/1975	Harms, Jr. et al.	
4,002,886 A	1/1977	Sundelin	
4,042,792 A	8/1977	Pakenham et al.	
4,365,148 A	12/1982	Whitney	
4,471,218 A	9/1984	Culp	
4,538,174 A	8/1985	Gargini et al.	
4,546,352 A	10/1985	Goldman	
4,581,484 A	4/1986	Bendig	
4,621,259 A	11/1986	Schepers et al.	
4,642,790 A	2/1987	Minshull et al.	
4,654,482 A	3/1987	DeAngelis	
4,672,377 A	6/1987	Murphy et al.	
4,710,727 A	12/1987	Rutt	
4,780,599 A	10/1988	Baus	
4,783,648 A	11/1988	Homma et al.	
4,785,296 A	11/1988	Tabata et al.	
4,789,147 A	12/1988	Berger et al.	
4,816,904 A	3/1989	McKenna et al.	
4,817,136 A	3/1989	Rhoads	
4,823,108 A	4/1989	Pope	
4,823,303 A	4/1989	Terasawa	
4,833,308 A	5/1989	Humble	
4,841,132 A	6/1989	Kajitani et al.	
4,845,634 A	7/1989	Vitek et al.	
4,850,009 A	7/1989	Zook et al.	
4,866,431 A	9/1989	Andros et al.	
4,890,098 A	12/1989	Dawes et al.	
4,893,333 A	1/1990	Baran et al.	
4,894,789 A	1/1990	Yee	
4,896,148 A	1/1990	Kurita	
4,899,370 A	2/1990	Kameo et al.	
4,901,073 A	2/1990	Kibrick	
4,905,094 A	2/1990	Pocock et al.	
4,907,264 A	3/1990	Seiler et al.	
4,916,293 A	4/1990	Cartlidge et al.	
4,937,853 A	6/1990	Brule et al.	
4,947,028 A *	8/1990	Gorog	235/380
4,959,530 A	9/1990	O'Connor	
4,972,504 A	11/1990	Daniel et al.	
4,975,948 A	12/1990	Andresen et al.	
4,982,346 A	1/1991	Girouard et al.	
4,983,817 A	1/1991	Dolash et al.	
4,984,155 A	1/1991	Geier et al.	
5,003,384 A	3/1991	Durden et al.	
5,038,023 A	8/1991	Saliga	
5,039,075 A	8/1991	Mayer	
5,047,614 A	9/1991	Bianco	
5,054,096 A	10/1991	Beizer	
5,060,170 A	10/1991	Bourgeois et al.	
5,088,045 A	2/1992	Shimanaka et al.	
5,111,391 A	5/1992	Fields et al.	
5,115,326 A	5/1992	Burgess et al.	
5,128,752 A	7/1992	Von Kohorn	
5,133,011 A	7/1992	McKiel, Jr.	
5,144,654 A	9/1992	Kelley et al.	
5,161,037 A	11/1992	Saito	
5,161,214 A	11/1992	Addink et al.	
5,175,422 A	12/1992	Koizumi et al.	
5,179,700 A	1/1993	Aihara et al.	
5,182,705 A	1/1993	Barr et al.	
5,189,630 A	2/1993	Barstow et al.	
5,191,525 A	3/1993	LeBrun et al.	
5,198,644 A	3/1993	Pfeiffer et al.	
5,213,337 A	5/1993	Sherman	
5,227,771 A	7/1993	Kerr et al.	
5,233,171 A	8/1993	Baldwin	
5,235,654 A	8/1993	Anderson et al.	
5,241,402 A	8/1993	Aboujaoude et al.	
5,243,531 A	9/1993	DiPippo et al.	
5,247,347 A	9/1993	Litteral et al.	
5,249,044 A	9/1993	Von Kohorn	
5,250,789 A	10/1993	Johnsen	
5,262,860 A	11/1993	Fitzpatrick et al.	
5,280,498 A	1/1994	Tymes et al.	
5,285,278 A	2/1994	Holman	
5,287,181 A *	2/1994	Holman	348/473
5,288,976 A	2/1994	Citron et al.	
5,296,688 A	3/1994	Hamilton et al.	
5,304,786 A	4/1994	Pavlidis et al.	
5,305,195 A	4/1994	Murphy	
5,319,454 A	6/1994	Schutte	
5,319,455 A	6/1994	Hoarty et al.	
5,324,922 A	6/1994	Roberts	
5,331,547 A	7/1994	Laszlo	
5,340,966 A	8/1994	Morimoto	
5,341,505 A	8/1994	Whitehouse	
5,349,678 A	9/1994	Morris et al.	
5,354,977 A	10/1994	Roustaei	
5,355,146 A	10/1994	Chiu et al.	
5,357,276 A	10/1994	Banker et al.	
5,359,367 A	10/1994	Stockill	
5,361,871 A	11/1994	Gupta et al.	
5,362,948 A	11/1994	Morimoto	
5,372,334 A	12/1994	Cuadros	
5,377,323 A	12/1994	Vasudevan	
5,382,779 A	1/1995	Gupta	
5,382,948 A	1/1995	Richmond	
5,386,298 A	1/1995	Bronnenberg et al.	
5,398,336 A	3/1995	Tantry et al.	
5,405,232 A	4/1995	Lloyd et al.	
5,418,713 A *	5/1995	Allen	705/32
5,420,403 A	5/1995	Allum et al.	
5,420,943 A	5/1995	Mak	
5,422,879 A *	6/1995	Parsons et al.	370/236
5,424,524 A	6/1995	Ruppert et al.	
5,426,427 A	6/1995	Chinnock et al.	
5,431,250 A	7/1995	Schlamp	
5,438,355 A	8/1995	Palmer	
5,442,749 A	8/1995	Northcutt et al.	
5,446,490 A	8/1995	Blahut et al.	
5,446,919 A	8/1995	Wilkins	
5,457,307 A	10/1995	Dumont	
5,465,291 A	11/1995	Barrus et al.	
5,483,052 A	1/1996	Smith et al.	
5,483,640 A	1/1996	Isfeld et al.	
5,491,495 A	2/1996	Ward et al.	
5,491,508 A	2/1996	Friedell et al.	
5,493,107 A	2/1996	Gupta et al.	
5,507,009 A	4/1996	Grube et al.	
5,519,878 A	5/1996	Dolin, Jr.	
5,523,982 A	6/1996	Dale	
5,530,852 A	6/1996	Meske, Jr. et al.	
5,532,773 A	7/1996	Shaw et al.	
5,548,110 A	8/1996	Storch et al.	
5,563,630 A	10/1996	Tsakiris et al.	
5,570,295 A	10/1996	Isenberg et al.	
5,572,643 A	11/1996	Judson	
5,578,818 A	11/1996	Kain et al.	
5,579,124 A	11/1996	Aijala et al.	
5,586,313 A	12/1996	Schnittker et al.	
5,590,197 A	12/1996	Chen et al.	
5,592,551 A	1/1997	Lett et al.	
5,594,226 A	1/1997	Steger	
5,595,264 A	1/1997	Trotta, Jr.	
5,600,779 A	2/1997	Palmer et al.	
5,602,377 A	2/1997	Beller et al.	
5,604,542 A	2/1997	Dedrick	
5,621,203 A	4/1997	Swartz et al.	
5,633,484 A	5/1997	Zancho et al.	
5,633,489 A	5/1997	Dvorkis et al.	
5,636,346 A	6/1997	Saxe	
5,640,002 A	6/1997	Ruppert et al.	
5,640,193 A	6/1997	Wellner	
5,646,390 A	7/1997	Wang et al.	
5,649,186 A	7/1997	Ferguson	
5,659,800 A	8/1997	Zhang et al.	
5,664,110 A	9/1997	Green et al.	
5,666,293 A	9/1997	Metz et al.	
5,671,226 A	9/1997	Murakami et al.	
5,671,282 A	9/1997	Wolff et al.	
5,673,322 A	9/1997	Pepe et al.	
5,675,721 A	10/1997	Freedman et al.	
5,682,540 A	10/1997	Klotz, Jr. et al.	
5,687,331 A	11/1997	Volk et al.	
5,694,163 A	12/1997	Harrison	
5,701,161 A	12/1997	Williams et al.	
5,704,029 A	12/1997	Wright, Jr.	

5,708,478 A	1/1998	Tognazzini	
5,708,780 A	1/1998	Levergood et al.	
5,710,887 A	1/1998	Chelliah et al.	
5,715,314 A	2/1998	Payne et al.	
5,721,848 A	2/1998	Joseph	
5,724,424 A	3/1998	Gifford	
5,726,898 A	3/1998	Jacobs	
5,729,002 A	3/1998	Samples	
5,732,218 A	3/1998	Bland et al.	
5,734,413 A	3/1998	Lappington et al.	
5,737,532 A	4/1998	DeLair et al.	
5,737,619 A	4/1998	Judson	
5,740,369 A	4/1998	Yokozawa et al.	
5,742,825 A	4/1998	Mather et al.	
5,745,681 A	4/1998	Levine et al.	
5,746,602 A	5/1998	Kikinis	
5,751,956 A	5/1998	Kirsch	
5,754,906 A	5/1998	Yoshida	
5,754,981 A	5/1998	Veeneman et al.	
5,757,917 A	5/1998	Rose et al.	
5,758,257 A	5/1998	Herz et al.	
5,761,606 A	6/1998	Wolzien	
5,761,648 A	6/1998	Golden et al.	
5,764,906 A	6/1998	Edelstein et al.	
5,765,176 A	6/1998	Bloomberg	
5,768,508 A	6/1998	Eikeland	
5,768,528 A	6/1998	Stumm	
5,768,539 A	6/1998	Metz et al.	
5,768,583 A	6/1998	Orzol et al.	
5,774,170 A	6/1998	Hite et al.	
5,774,534 A	6/1998	Mayer	
5,774,660 A	6/1998	Brendel et al.	
5,774,664 A	6/1998	Hidary et al.	
5,774,666 A	6/1998	Portuesi	
5,774,870 A	6/1998	Storey	
5,774,874 A	6/1998	Veeneman et al.	
5,778,181 A	7/1998	Hidary et al.	
5,778,367 A	7/1998	Wesinger, Jr. et al.	
5,786,585 A	7/1998	Eastman et al.	
5,787,246 A	7/1998	Lichtman et al.	
5,790,793 A	8/1998	Higley	
5,791,991 A	8/1998	Small	
5,794,210 A	8/1998	Goldhaber et al.	
5,796,952 A	8/1998	Davis et al.	
5,801,067 A	9/1998	Shaw et al.	
5,804,803 A	9/1998	Cragun et al.	
5,805,154 A	9/1998	Brown	
5,805,806 A	9/1998	McArthur	
5,806,044 A	9/1998	Powell	
5,812,776 A	9/1998	Gifford	
5,815,776 A	9/1998	Nukada	
5,818,438 A	10/1998	Howe et al.	
5,818,440 A	10/1998	Allibhoy et al.	
5,818,441 A	10/1998	Throckmorton et al.	
5,818,935 A	10/1998	Maa	
5,822,436 A	10/1998	Rhoads	
5,825,009 A	10/1998	Schmid et al.	
5,826,000 A	10/1998	Hamilton	
5,826,064 A	10/1998	Loring et al.	
5,826,166 A	10/1998	Brooks et al.	
5,831,261 A	11/1998	Plesko	
5,832,223 A	11/1998	Hara et al.	
5,832,432 A	11/1998	Trader et al.	
5,832,449 A	11/1998	Cunningham	
5,833,468 A	11/1998	Guy et al.	
5,835,861 A	11/1998	Whiteside	
5,835,911 A	11/1998	Nakagawa et al.	
5,842,178 A	11/1998	Giovannoli	
5,848,202 A	12/1998	D'Eri et al.	
5,848,292 A	12/1998	Nathan	
5,848,397 A	12/1998	Marsh et al.	
5,848,413 A	12/1998	Wolff	
5,848,426 A	12/1998	Wang et al.	
5,850,187 A	12/1998	Carrender et al.	
5,854,897 A	12/1998	Radziewicz et al.	
5,854,945 A	12/1998	Criscito et al.	
5,862,452 A	1/1999	Cudak et al.	
5,864,823 A	1/1999	Levitan	
5,867,730 A	2/1999	Leyda	
5,869,819 A	2/1999	Knowles et al.	
5,870,546 A	2/1999	Kursch	
5,872,588 A	2/1999	Aras et al.	
5,874,722 A	2/1999	Rando et al.	
5,875,327 A	2/1999	Brandt et al.	
5,875,415 A	2/1999	Lieb et al.	
5,878,416 A *	3/1999	Harris et al.	705/28
5,880,769 A	3/1999	Nemirofsky et al.	
5,884,014 A	3/1999	Huttenlocher et al.	
5,886,634 A	3/1999	Muhme	
5,887,176 A	3/1999	Griffith et al.	
5,887,243 A	3/1999	Harvey et al.	
5,894,516 A	4/1999	Brandenburg	
5,903,225 A	5/1999	Schmitt et al.	
5,903,721 A	5/1999	Sixtus	
5,905,248 A	5/1999	Russell et al.	
5,905,251 A	5/1999	Knowles	
5,905,521 A	5/1999	Gatto et al.	
5,905,665 A	5/1999	Rim	
5,905,865 A	5/1999	Palmer et al.	
5,907,322 A	5/1999	Kelly et al.	
5,907,793 A	5/1999	Reams	
5,909,183 A	6/1999	Borgstahl et al.	
5,912,454 A	6/1999	Castillo et al.	
5,913,210 A	6/1999	Call	
5,915,090 A	6/1999	Joseph et al.	
5,916,024 A	6/1999	Von Kohorn	
5,917,725 A	6/1999	Thacher et al.	
5,918,211 A	6/1999	Sloane	
5,918,213 A	6/1999	Bernard et al.	
5,918,214 A	6/1999	Perkowski	
5,923,735 A	7/1999	Swartz et al.	
5,923,806 A	7/1999	Sugawara	
5,925,865 A	7/1999	Steger	
5,929,849 A	7/1999	Kikinis	
5,929,850 A	7/1999	Broadwin et al.	
5,930,767 A	7/1999	Reber et al.	
5,932,863 A	8/1999	Rathus et al.	
5,933,811 A	8/1999	Angles et al.	
5,933,829 A	8/1999	Durst et al.	
5,935,004 A	8/1999	Tarr et al.	
5,937,163 A	8/1999	Lee et al.	
5,938,726 A	8/1999	Reber et al.	
5,938,727 A	8/1999	Ikeda	
5,940,073 A	8/1999	Klosternan et al.	
5,943,432 A	8/1999	Gilmore et al.	
5,944,791 A	8/1999	Scherpbier	
5,946,103 A	8/1999	Curry	
5,947,746 A	9/1999	Tsai	
5,948,061 A	9/1999	Merriman et al.	
5,950,173 A	9/1999	Perkowski	
5,951,639 A	9/1999	MacInnis	
5,956,699 A	9/1999	Wong et al.	
5,957,695 A	9/1999	Redford et al.	
5,959,275 A	9/1999	Hughes et al.	
5,960,411 A	9/1999	Hartman et al.	
5,961,603 A	10/1999	Kunkel et al.	
5,963,916 A	10/1999	Kaplan	
5,963,926 A	10/1999	Kumomura	
5,970,469 A	10/1999	Scroggie et al.	
5,970,471 A	10/1999	Hill	
5,970,472 A	10/1999	Allsop et al.	
5,971,277 A	10/1999	Cragun et al.	
5,973,684 A	10/1999	Brooks et al.	
5,974,443 A	10/1999	Jeske	
5,974,451 A	10/1999	Simmons	
5,976,833 A	11/1999	Furukawa et al.	
5,978,773 A *	11/1999	Hudetz et al.	705/23
5,979,757 A	11/1999	Tracy et al.	
5,986,651 A	11/1999	Reber et al.	
5,987,507 A	11/1999	Creedon et al.	
5,987,509 A	11/1999	Portuesi	
5,991,601 A *	11/1999	Anderson	340/7.1
5,991,739 A	11/1999	Cupps et al.	
5,991,749 A	11/1999	Morrill, Jr.	
5,992,744 A	11/1999	Smith et al.	
5,992,752 A	11/1999	Wilz, Sr. et al.	
5,995,105 A	11/1999	Reber et al.	
5,995,965 A	11/1999	Experton	

5,996,022	A	11/1999	Krueger et al.	6,148,301	A	11/2000	Rosenthal
5,996,896	A	12/1999	Grabon	6,148,331	A	11/2000	Parry
5,999,996	A	12/1999	Dunn	6,148,405	A	11/2000	Liao et al.
6,002,394	A	12/1999	Schein et al.	6,149,063	A	11/2000	Reynolds et al.
6,002,852	A	12/1999	Birdwell et al.	6,151,624	A	11/2000	Teare et al.
6,002,946	A	12/1999	Reber et al.	6,152,369	A	11/2000	Wilz, Sr. et al.
6,003,014	A	12/1999	Lee et al.	6,154,738	A	11/2000	Call
6,003,073	A	12/1999	Solvason	6,154,771	A	11/2000	Rangan et al.
6,005,939	A	12/1999	Fortenberry et al.	6,161,132	A	12/2000	Roberts et al.
6,006,257	A	12/1999	Slezak	6,163,803	A	12/2000	Watanabe
6,009,274	A	12/1999	Fletcher et al.	6,167,567	A	12/2000	Chiles et al.
6,009,410	A	12/1999	LeMole et al.	6,169,484	B1	1/2001	Schuchman et al.
6,009,465	A	12/1999	Decker et al.	6,170,746	B1	1/2001	Brook et al.
6,012,038	A	1/2000	Powell	6,177,860	B1	1/2001	Cromer et al.
6,012,045	A	1/2000	Barzilai et al.	6,178,443	B1	1/2001	Lin
6,012,102	A	1/2000	Shachar	6,181,351	B1	1/2001	Merrill et al.
6,014,090	A	1/2000	Rosen et al.	6,185,542	B1	2/2001	Moran et al.
6,014,634	A	1/2000	Scroggie et al.	6,185,589	B1	2/2001	Votipka
6,014,641	A	1/2000	Loeb et al.	6,188,398	B1	2/2001	Collins-Rector et al.
6,014,701	A	1/2000	Chaddha	6,189,050	B1	2/2001	Sakarda
6,015,167	A	1/2000	Savino et al.	6,192,380	B1	2/2001	Light et al.
6,018,764	A	1/2000	Field et al.	6,192,400	B1	2/2001	Hanson et al.
6,023,255	A	2/2000	Bell	6,195,420	B1	2/2001	Tognauini
6,024,641	A	2/2000	Sarno	6,195,693	B1	2/2001	Berry et al.
6,026,376	A	2/2000	Kenney	6,199,048	B1	3/2001	Hudetz et al.
6,029,045	A	2/2000	Picco et al.	6,199,079	B1	3/2001	Gupta et al.
6,029,196	A	2/2000	Lenz	6,202,054	B1	3/2001	Lawlor et al.
6,032,195	A	2/2000	Reber et al.	6,202,062	B1	3/2001	Cameron et al.
6,037,928	A	3/2000	Nachinson et al.	6,220,509	B1	4/2001	Byford
6,037,934	A	3/2000	Himmel et al.	6,223,029	B1	4/2001	Stenman et al.
6,038,366	A	3/2000	Ohno	6,226,618	B1	5/2001	Downs et al.
6,044,362	A	3/2000	Neely	6,230,325	B1	5/2001	Iinuma et al.
6,045,048	A	4/2000	Wilz et al.	6,233,565	B1	5/2001	Lewis et al.
6,049,539	A	4/2000	Lee et al.	6,233,736	B1	5/2001	Wolzien
6,049,870	A	4/2000	Greaves	6,236,836	B1	5/2001	Westman et al.
6,055,573	A	4/2000	Gardenswartz et al.	6,237,025	B1	5/2001	Ludwig et al.
6,061,368	A	5/2000	Hitzelberger	6,238,290	B1	5/2001	Tarr et al.
6,061,440	A	5/2000	Delaney et al.	6,240,448	B1	5/2001	Imielinski et al.
6,061,646	A	5/2000	Martino et al.	6,243,814	B1	6/2001	Matena
6,061,660	A	5/2000	Eggleston et al.	6,247,047	B1	6/2001	Wolff
6,061,719	A	5/2000	Bendinelli et al.	6,247,128	B1	6/2001	Fisher et al.
6,064,804	A	5/2000	Bring et al.	6,249,810	B1	6/2001	Kiraly
6,064,929	A	5/2000	Migues et al.	6,251,016	B1	6/2001	Tsuda et al.
6,064,979	A	5/2000	Perkowski	6,251,017	B1	6/2001	Leason et al.
6,067,526	A	5/2000	Powell	6,256,498	B1	7/2001	Ludwig
6,070,147	A	5/2000	Harms et al.	6,256,732	B1	7/2001	Cromer et al.
6,070,160	A	5/2000	Geary	6,260,023	B1	7/2001	Seevers et al.
6,070,798	A	6/2000	Nethery	6,263,383	B1	7/2001	Lee et al.
6,073,119	A	6/2000	Bornemisza-Wahr et al.	6,278,717	B1	8/2001	Arsenault et al.
6,073,851	A	6/2000	Olmstead et al.	6,279,830	B1	8/2001	Ishibashi
6,076,166	A	6/2000	Moshfeghi et al.	6,282,522	B1	8/2001	Davis et al.
6,076,733	A	6/2000	Wilz, Sr. et al.	6,282,713	B1	8/2001	Kitsukawa et al.
6,078,321	A	6/2000	Simonoff et al.	6,290,131	B1	9/2001	Kolis et al.
6,081,629	A	6/2000	Browning	6,292,786	B1	9/2001	Deaton et al.
6,084,523	A	7/2000	Gelnovatch et al.	6,297,727	B1	10/2001	Nelson, Jr.
6,085,146	A	7/2000	Kuribayashi et al.	6,297,819	B1	10/2001	Furst
6,085,247	A	7/2000	Parsons, Jr. et al.	6,298,373	B1	10/2001	Burns et al.
6,097,375	A	8/2000	Byford	6,300,872	B1	10/2001	Mathias et al.
6,098,106	A	8/2000	Philyaw et al.	6,301,012	B1	10/2001	White et al.
6,101,483	A	8/2000	Petrovich et al.	6,301,612	B1	10/2001	Selitrennikoff et al.
6,104,845	A	8/2000	Lipman et al.	6,308,893	B1	10/2001	Waxelbaum et al.
6,108,656	A	8/2000	Durst et al.	6,311,165	B1	10/2001	Coutts et al.
6,108,706	A	8/2000	Birdwell et al.	6,311,185	B1	10/2001	Markowitz et al.
6,112,323	A	8/2000	Meizlik et al.	6,311,214	B1	10/2001	Rhoads
6,112,981	A	9/2000	McCall	6,311,896	B1	11/2001	Mulla et al.
6,114,712	A	9/2000	Dvorkis et al.	6,314,451	B1	11/2001	Landsman et al.
6,119,944	A	9/2000	Mulla et al.	6,314,456	B1	11/2001	Van Andel et al.
6,122,403	A	9/2000	Rhoads	6,317,761	B1	11/2001	Landsman et al.
6,122,740	A	9/2000	Andersen	6,317,780	B1	11/2001	Cohn et al.
6,123,259	A	9/2000	Ogasawara	6,317,789	B1	11/2001	Rakavy et al.
6,123,263	A	9/2000	Feng	6,317,791	B1	11/2001	Cohn et al.
6,131,116	A	10/2000	Riggins et al.	6,317,885	B1	11/2001	Fries
6,133,849	A	10/2000	McConnell et al.	6,321,991	B1	11/2001	Knowles
6,134,532	A	10/2000	Lazarus et al.	6,321,992	B1	11/2001	Knowles et al.
6,134,548	A	10/2000	Gottsman et al.	6,324,519	B1	11/2001	Eldering
6,134,616	A	10/2000	Beatty	6,327,574	B1	12/2001	Kramer et al.
6,138,036	A	10/2000	O'Cinneide	6,328,213	B1	12/2001	He et al.
6,138,155	A	10/2000	Davis et al.	6,330,543	B1	12/2001	Kepecs
6,144,848	A	11/2000	Walsh et al.	6,330,593	B1	12/2001	Roberts et al.

6,330,595 B1	12/2001	Ullman et al.	
6,330,669 B1	12/2001	McKeeth	
6,330,715 B1	12/2001	Razzaghe-Ashrafi	
6,331,972 B1	12/2001	Harris et al.	
6,334,113 B1	12/2001	Walker et al.	
6,336,152 B1	1/2002	Richman et al.	
6,337,717 B1	1/2002	Nason et al.	
6,338,094 B1	1/2002	Scott et al.	
6,343,276 B1	1/2002	Barnett	
6,351,467 B1	2/2002	Dillon	
6,351,640 B1	2/2002	DeMont	
6,353,898 B1	3/2002	Wipfel et al.	
6,353,926 B1	3/2002	Parthesarathy et al.	
6,353,929 B1	3/2002	Houston	
6,356,876 B1	3/2002	Lingham	
6,356,949 B1	3/2002	Katsandres et al.	
6,357,042 B2	3/2002	Srinivasan et al.	
6,359,711 B1	3/2002	Cole et al.	
6,368,177 B1	4/2002	Gabai et al.	
6,374,237 B1	4/2002	Reese	
6,374,402 B1	4/2002	Schmeidler et al.	
6,377,690 B1	4/2002	Witschorik	
6,377,930 B1	4/2002	Chen et al.	
6,377,983 B1	4/2002	Cohen et al.	
6,377,986 B1	4/2002	Philyaw et al.	
6,381,632 B1	4/2002	Lowell	
6,384,744 B1	5/2002	Philyaw et al.	
6,386,454 B2	5/2002	Hecht et al.	
6,389,409 B1	5/2002	Horovitz et al.	
6,389,464 B1	5/2002	Krishnamurthy et al.	
6,393,297 B1	5/2002	Song	
6,394,354 B1	5/2002	Wilz et al.	
6,398,106 B1	6/2002	Ulvr et al.	
6,400,272 B1	6/2002	Holtzman et al.	
6,400,407 B1	6/2002	Zigmond et al.	
6,401,059 B1	6/2002	Shen et al.	
6,401,077 B1	6/2002	Godden et al.	
6,404,435 B1	6/2002	Miller et al.	
6,405,049 B2	6/2002	Herrod et al.	
6,412,699 B1	7/2002	Russell et al.	
6,415,438 B1	7/2002	Blackketter et al.	
6,415,439 B1	7/2002	Randell et al.	
6,415,983 B1	7/2002	Ulvr et al.	
6,418,441 B1	7/2002	Call	
6,418,555 B2	7/2002	Mohammed	
6,421,445 B1	7/2002	Jensen et al.	
6,421,732 B1	7/2002	Alkhatib et al.	
6,424,249 B1	7/2002	Houvener	
6,427,238 B1	7/2002	Goodman et al.	
6,430,554 B1	8/2002	Rothschild	
6,430,743 B1	8/2002	Matsuura	
6,434,530 B1	8/2002	Sloane et al.	
6,442,529 B1	8/2002	Krishan et al.	
6,442,530 B1	8/2002	Miller	
6,446,049 B1	9/2002	Janning et al.	
6,446,119 B1	9/2002	Olah et al.	
6,446,871 B1	9/2002	Buckley et al.	
6,449,518 B1	9/2002	Yokoo et al.	
6,459,439 B1	10/2002	Ahlquist et al.	
6,460,093 B1	10/2002	Taugher	
6,463,416 B1	10/2002	Messina	
6,463,420 B1	10/2002	Guidice et al.	
6,469,689 B1	10/2002	Dow et al.	
6,484,022 B1	11/2002	Findikli et al.	
6,484,149 B1	11/2002	Jammes et al.	
6,484,198 B1	11/2002	Milovanovic et al.	
6,487,538 B1	11/2002	Gupta et al.	
6,487,719 B1	11/2002	Itoh et al.	
6,490,601 B1	12/2002	Markus et al.	
6,490,637 B1	12/2002	Shih	
6,493,770 B1	12/2002	Sartore et al.	
6,496,858 B1	12/2002	Frailong et al.	
6,496,981 B1	12/2002	Wistendahl et al.	
6,501,854 B1	12/2002	Konishi et al.	
6,502,242 B1	12/2002	Howe et al.	
6,504,626 B1	1/2003	Shih	
6,510,997 B1	1/2003	Wilz et al.	
6,512,522 B1	1/2003	Miller et al.	
6,513,717 B2	2/2003	Hannigan	
6,517,002 B1	2/2003	Piatek	
6,519,463 B2	2/2003	Tendler	
6,526,449 B1	2/2003	Philyaw et al.	
6,536,666 B1	3/2003	Hudrick	
6,536,670 B1	3/2003	Postman et al.	
6,540,144 B1	4/2003	Hudrick et al.	
6,542,874 B1	4/2003	Walker et al.	
6,542,933 B1	4/2003	Durst et al.	
6,542,943 B2	4/2003	Cheng et al.	
6,543,052 B1	4/2003	Ogasawara	
6,546,418 B2	4/2003	Schena et al.	
6,560,640 B2	5/2003	Smethers	
6,577,861 B2	6/2003	Ogasawara	
6,577,877 B1	6/2003	Charlier et al.	
6,580,870 B1	6/2003	Kanazawa et al.	
6,581,838 B1	6/2003	Meksavan et al.	
6,584,459 B1	6/2003	Chang et al.	
6,587,835 B1	7/2003	Treyz et al.	
6,591,247 B2	7/2003	Stern	
6,594,705 B1	7/2003	Philyaw	
6,595,859 B2	7/2003	Lynn	
6,600,418 B2	7/2003	Francis et al.	
6,600,496 B1	7/2003	Wagner et al.	
6,600,725 B1	7/2003	Roy	
6,601,172 B1	7/2003	Epstein	
6,604,242 B1	8/2003	Weinstein et al.	
6,604,681 B1	8/2003	Burke et al.	
6,612,495 B2	9/2003	Reddersen et al.	
6,615,268 B1	9/2003	Philyaw et al.	
6,616,056 B2	9/2003	Cato	
6,622,165 B1	9/2003	Philyaw	
6,625,581 B1	9/2003	Perkowski	
6,636,896 B1	10/2003	Philyaw	
6,637,028 B1	10/2003	Voyticky et al.	
6,645,068 B1	11/2003	Kelly et al.	
6,661,904 B1	12/2003	Sasich et al.	
6,665,836 B1	12/2003	Wynblatt et al.	
6,668,133 B2	12/2003	Yuen et al.	
6,668,293 B2	12/2003	Chen et al.	
6,678,866 B1	1/2004	Sugimoto et al.	
6,686,910 B2	2/2004	O'Donnell, Jr.	
6,688,522 B1	2/2004	Philyaw et al.	
6,697,949 B1	2/2004	Philyaw et al.	
6,701,354 B1	3/2004	Philyaw et al.	
6,701,369 B1 *	3/2004	Philyaw	709/229
6,701,524 B1	3/2004	Okamura et al.	
6,704,864 B1	3/2004	Philyaw	
6,708,208 B1	3/2004	Philyaw	
6,725,260 B1	4/2004	Philyaw	
6,725,461 B1	4/2004	Dougherty et al.	
6,738,978 B1	5/2004	Hendricks et al.	
6,741,574 B2	5/2004	Arsenault	
6,745,234 B1	6/2004	Philyaw et al.	
6,748,278 B1	6/2004	Maymudes	
6,753,883 B2	6/2004	Schena et al.	
6,758,398 B1	7/2004	Philyaw et al.	
6,778,096 B1	8/2004	Ward et al.	
6,779,178 B1	8/2004	Lloyd et al.	
6,785,659 B1	8/2004	Landsman et al.	
6,791,588 B1	9/2004	Philyaw	
6,792,452 B1	9/2004	Philyaw	
6,792,618 B1	9/2004	Bendinelli et al.	
6,806,808 B1	10/2004	Watters et al.	
6,813,608 B1	11/2004	Baranowski	
6,813,776 B2	11/2004	Chernock et al.	
6,816,894 B1	11/2004	Philyaw et al.	
6,823,366 B1	11/2004	Nakano	
6,826,775 B1	11/2004	Howe et al.	
6,829,646 B1	12/2004	Philyaw et al.	
6,829,650 B1	12/2004	Philyaw et al.	
6,832,729 B1	12/2004	Perry et al.	
6,836,799 B1	12/2004	Philyaw et al.	
6,837,436 B2	1/2005	Swartz et al.	
6,843,417 B1	1/2005	Philyaw et al.	
6,845,388 B1	1/2005	Philyaw	
6,857,131 B1	2/2005	Yagawa et al.	
6,859,699 B2	2/2005	Carroll et al.	
6,877,032 B1	4/2005	Philyaw	
6,886,013 B1	4/2005	Beranek	

6,886,178	B1	4/2005	Mao et al.
6,892,226	B1	5/2005	Tso et al.
6,961,555	B1	11/2005	Philyaw
6,961,712	B1	11/2005	Perkowski
6,970,916	B1	11/2005	Philyaw
6,985,954	B1	1/2006	Philyaw et al.
6,988,248	B1	1/2006	Tang et al.
6,990,680	B1	1/2006	Wugofski
7,069,582	B2	6/2006	Philyaw et al.
7,092,768	B1	8/2006	Labuda
7,110,981	B1	9/2006	Sidikman et al.
7,159,037	B1	1/2007	Philyaw et al.
7,194,259	B2	3/2007	DeLine
7,200,865	B1	4/2007	Roscoe et al.
7,272,155	B2	9/2007	Kenney et al.
7,308,483	B2	12/2007	Philyaw
7,328,045	B2	2/2008	Funk et al.
7,370,114	B1	5/2008	Philyaw et al.
7,421,728	B2	9/2008	Zigmond et al.
7,441,710	B2 *	10/2008	Perkowski 235/492
7,505,785	B2 *	3/2009	Callaghan et al. 455/557
7,571,178	B2 *	8/2009	Watanabe et al. 1/1
2001/0044808	A1 *	11/2001	Milewski et al. 707/204
2002/0016770	A1	2/2002	Flenley et al.
2002/0059139	A1	5/2002	Evans
2002/0059241	A1	5/2002	Van Ryzin
2003/0149663	A1 *	8/2003	Vonholm et al. 705/39
2003/0212570	A1 *	11/2003	Chu et al. 705/1
2005/0021671	A1 *	1/2005	Philyaw et al. 709/217
2008/0015887	A1 *	1/2008	Drabek et al. 705/1
2008/0077527	A1 *	3/2008	Choe et al. 705/44

FOREIGN PATENT DOCUMENTS

EP	0837406	4/1998
EP	0927945 A2	7/1999
JP	10078928	3/1998
JP	10124428	5/1998
JP	10134117	5/1998
JP	10171758	6/1998
JP	10188140	7/1998
WO	WO 95/28044	10/1995
WO	WO 97/33434 A1	9/1997
WO	WO 98/19259	5/1998
WO	WO 98/26548	6/1998
WO	WO 98/57490	12/1998
WO	WO 99/38321	7/1999
WO	WO 00/16205	3/2000

OTHER PUBLICATIONS

Edwards, W. Keith et al. "Systematic Output Modification in a 2D User Interface Toolkit," Proceedings of the 10th ACM Symposium on User Interface Software and Technology (UIST '97) Oct. 14-17, 1997, pp. 1-8.

Gralla, Preston, How the Internet Works, Millennium Ed., Que Corporation, Aug. 8, 1999.

Hinton, William Frederick, et al.; "Document on Computer;" IPCC96 Fast Track, May 1996, IEEE, pp. 132-144.

White, Ron, How Computers Work, Millennium Ed. Que Corporation; Sep. 1999.

Johnston, A.G.; "What do Forward Looking Companies Consider in their Plans and Developments?;" Nestle; IEE Colloquium, Oct. 12, 1997, pp. 4/1 to 4/4.

Mikio Kuroki et al.; "Bar-code Recognition System Using Image Processing;" Hitachi Research Laboratory, Ltd.; pp. 568-572; no date.

Muller, Nathan J., Desktop Encyclopedia of the Internet, Artech House, Inc., 1998.

Neves, Ricardo and Noivo, Joao; "The Automation Synergy;" ISIE '97, Guimaraes, Portugal; 1997; pp. 49-52.

Taylor, Bernard W., III, Introduction to Management Science, 5th Ed., Prentice-Hall Inc., NJ, 1996.

The Bank Credit Card Business. 2nd Edition. American Bankers Association, 1996.

Thomas, James W. and Nagle, Joan G.; "Group Decision Support System: Development and Application", Energy Systems, Westinghouse Electric Corporation; Feb. 1989, IEEE, pp. 213-216.

White, James J. and Summers, Robert S. Uniform Commercial Code. 4th Ed. West Publishing Co., St. Paul MN, 1995.

* cited by examiner

FIG. 1

- ADVERTISER DATA INPUT —100
- AUDIO MODULATE —102
- TV PROGRAM SOURCE —104
- ⊗ —106
- 107
- 108 / 109 — 101
- RECEIVER —110
- 111
- AUDIO OUT —113
- 117
- DISPLAY —118
- PC —112
- MODEM —114 — TO NETWORK
- PROGRAM INFORMATION —116

FIG. 2

- 109
- RECEIVER —110
- 204
- SOUND CARD —206
- MODEM —208 — TO NETWORK
- CPU
- DISPLAY —118
- ADVERTISER WEB PAGE 212

FIG. 3

- 108
- RECEIVER —110
- 111
- PC —302
- NETWORK INTERFACE —304
- PC —300
- I/F
- PC —303
- I/F
- 306
- GLOBAL COMMUNICATION NETWORK
- A B C D
- E
- 308 ARS
- ADVERTISER DATABASE —310
- 314 ARS
- ADVERTISER DATABASE
- 312 ADVERTISER SERVER
- 316 ADVERTISER A SERVER

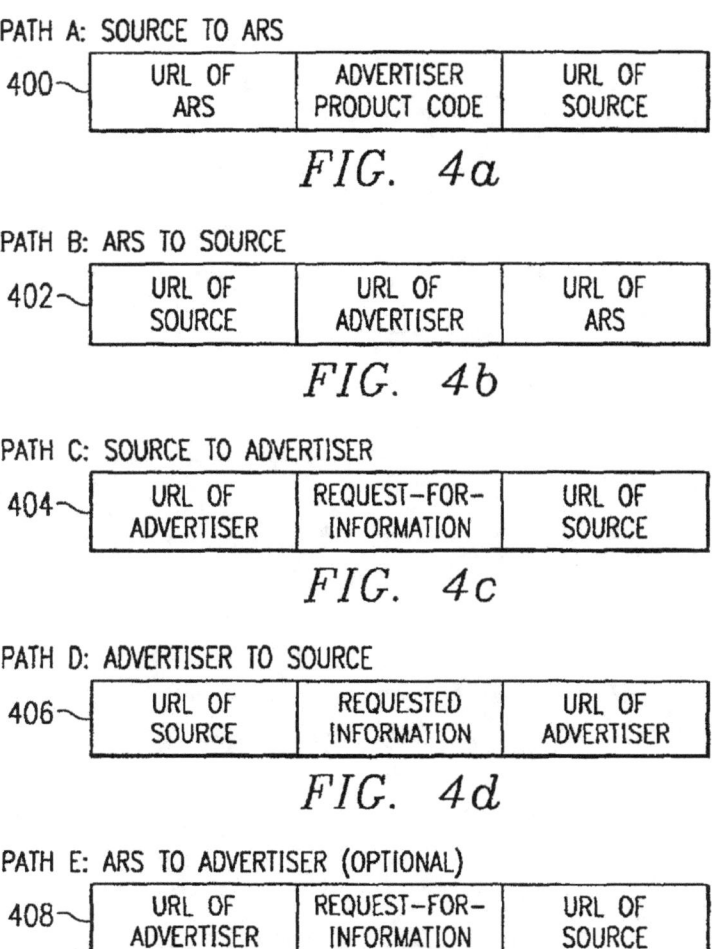

PATH A: SOURCE TO ARS

400 — | URL OF ARS | ADVERTISER PRODUCT CODE | URL OF SOURCE |

FIG. 4a

PATH B: ARS TO SOURCE

402 — | URL OF SOURCE | URL OF ADVERTISER | URL OF ARS |

FIG. 4b

PATH C: SOURCE TO ADVERTISER

404 — | URL OF ADVERTISER | REQUEST-FOR-INFORMATION | URL OF SOURCE |

FIG. 4c

PATH D: ADVERTISER TO SOURCE

406 — | URL OF SOURCE | REQUESTED INFORMATION | URL OF ADVERTISER |

FIG. 4d

PATH E: ARS TO ADVERTISER (OPTIONAL)

408 — | URL OF ADVERTISER | REQUEST-FOR-INFORMATION | URL OF SOURCE |

FIG. 4e

FIG. 6

FIG. 5

FIG. 7

DISPLAY

FIG. 8

FIG. 9

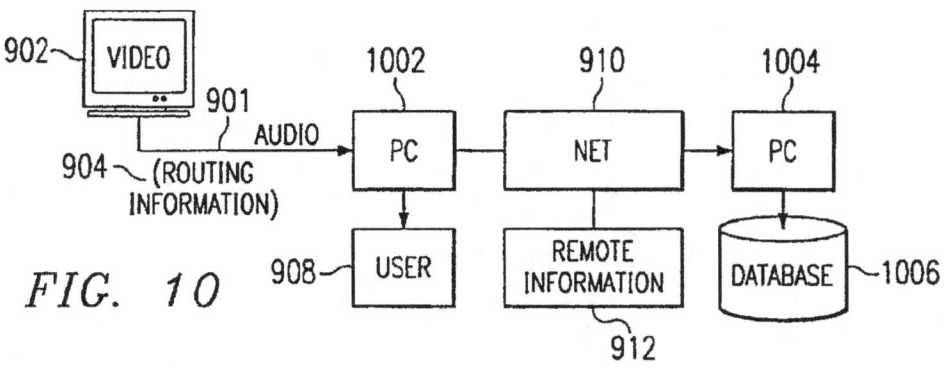

FIG. 10

PRIMARY ROUTING INFORMATION

FIG. 11

| PRIMARY ROUTING INFORMATION | SECONDARY ROUTING INFORMATION |

VIDEO SOURCE

OPTICAL REGION

902 → 1204 → 1202

SENSED VIDEO → PC → NET → REMOTE INFORMATION

906   910   912

908 → USER

FIG. 12

VIDEO — 902

901

904 — (ROUTING INFORMATION)

AUDIO

PROFILE DATABASE — 1302

ID — 1304

PC — 906

NET — 910

SUBSCRIBER — 1312

REMOTE INFORMATION — 912

908 — USER

ARS — 312

BILLING — 1316

INTERMEDIATE DESTINATION TABLES — 310

PROFILE DATABASE — 1308

TRANSACTION — 1310

FIG. 13

FIG. 14

FIG. 15

FIG. 16

FIG. 17

FIG. 18

FIG. 19

FIG. 20

FIG. 21

ARS DATABASE
2100

2102		2104		2106	2108	
PRODUCT		WAND		USER	E-COMMERCE	
BAR CODE	ROUTE	ID	DISTRIBUTOR	PROFILE	BAR CODE	INFORMATION

FIG. 22

USER

2200 — SCAN? — N

Y

2202 — ASSEMBLE BAR CODE, WAND ID, ARS URL AND LAUNCH BROWSER

2204 — WINDOW PARTITIONED INTO THREE FRAMES; WAND ID, BAR CODE AND E-COMMERCE

RECEIVE ROUTING? — N

2206 — Y

2208 — ROUTE INFORMATION FOR EACH WINDOW

2210 — RECEIVE INFORMATION FROM ROUTED-TO SITES

2212 — PLACE IN ASSIGNED FRAME

END

FIG. 23

ARS

2300 BAR CODE? N

Y

2302 MATCH TO MFG

2304 ASSEMBLE BAR CODE ROUTING STRING

2306 WAND ID? N

Y

2308 ASSEMBLE WAND ID ROUTING STRING

E-COMMERCE? N

2310 Y

2312 PROCESS AND ASSEMBLE E-COMMERCE ROUTING STRING

2314 RETURN ALL ROUTING STRINGS

END

FIG. 24

E-COMMERCE

RECEIVE MESSAGE PACKET 2400

2402 BAR CODE INFORMATION MATCHED? N 2404 REJECT

Y

MATCH BAR CODE WITH WAND ID 2406

LOOKUP E-COMMERCE ACTION 2408

ASSEMBLE MESSAGE PACKET WITH E-COMMERCE INFORMATION AND ROUTING INFORMATION (BAR CODE CONTENT AND/OR USER PROFILE) 2410

TRANSMIT TO USER PC 2412

RETURN

1

INPUT DEVICE FOR ALLOWING INTERFACE TO A WEB SITE IN ASSOCIATION WITH A UNIQUE INPUT CODE

CROSS-REFERENCE TO RELATED APPLICATIONS

This application is a Continuation of U.S. patent application Ser. No. 09/494,924, filed Feb. 1, 2000, now U.S. Pat. No. 7,428,499, issued on Sep. 23, 2008, and entitled, "INPUT DEVICE FOR ALLOWING INTERFACE TO A WEB SITE IN ASSOCIATION WITH A UNIQUE INPUT CODE," which is a Continuation of U.S. patent application Ser. No. 09/378,221 entitled "METHOD AND APPARATUS FOR ACCESSING A REMOTE LOCATION BY SCANNING AN OPTICAL CODE," filed on Aug. 19, 1999, now U.S. Pat. No. 6,745,234, issued on Jun. 1, 2004, which is a Continuation-in-Part of both U.S. patent application Ser. No. 09/151, 471 entitled "METHOD FOR INTERFACING SCANNED PRODUCT INFORMATION WITH A SOURCE FOR THE PRODUCT OVER A GLOBAL NETWORK" filed on Sep. 11, 1998, now abandoned and U.S. patent application Ser. No. 09/151,530 entitled "METHOD FOR CONTROLLING A COMPUTER WITH AN AUDIO SIGNAL" filed on Sep. 11, 1998, and which issued on Aug. 1, 2000 as U.S. Pat. No. 6,098,106.

TECHNICAL FIELD OF THE INVENTION

This invention is related to a method of computer control and, more particularly, to a system for automatically directing a web browser application on the computer to retrieve and display information in response to an analog signal.

BACKGROUND OF THE INVENTION

With the growing numbers of computer users connecting to the "Internet," many companies are seeking the substantial commercial opportunities presented by such a large user base. For example, one technology which exists allows a television ("TV") signal to trigger a computer response in which the consumer will be guided to a personalized web page. The source of the triggering signal may be a TV, video tape recorder, or radio. For example, if a viewer is watching a TV program in which an advertiser offers viewer voting, the advertiser may transmit a unique signal within the television signal which controls a program known as a "browser" on the viewer's computer to automatically display the advertiser's web page. The viewer then simply makes a selection which is then transmitted back to the advertiser.

In order to provide the viewer with the capability of responding to a wide variety of companies using this technology, a database of company information and Uniform Resource Locator ("URL") codes is necessarily maintained in the viewer's computer, requiring continuous updates. URLs are short strings of data that identify resources on the Internet: documents, images, downloadable files, services, electronic mailboxes, and other resources. URLs make resources available under a variety of naming schemes and access methods such as HTTP, FTP, and Internet mail, addressable in the same simple way. URLs reduce the tedium of "login to this server, then issue this magic command . . . " down to a single click. The Internet uses URLs to specify the location of files on other servers. A URL includes the type of resource being accessed (e.g., Web, gopher, FTP), the address of the server, and the location of the file. The URL can point

2

to any file on any networked computer. Current technology requires the viewer to perform periodic updates to obtain the most current URL database. This aspect of the current technology is cumbersome since the update process requires downloading information to the viewer's computer. Moreover, the likelihood for error in performing the update, and the necessity of redoing the update in the event of a later computer crash, further complicates the process. Additionally, current technologies are limited in the number of companies which may be stored in the database. This is a significant limitation since world-wide access presented by the Internet and the increasing number of companies connecting to perform on-line E-commerce necessitates a large database.

SUMMARY OF THE INVENTION

The present invention disclosed and claimed herein, in one aspect thereof, comprises a method for interconnecting a first location on a global communication network with a second location thereon. An input device is provided at the first location on the global communication network having associated therewith a unique input device ID. A product code disposed on a product is scanned with the input device, which product code is representative of the product in commercial transactions, the operation of scanning operable to extract the information contained in the product code to provide a unique value as an output. The unique value is then associated with the unique input device ID. In response to the operation of scanning and associating, the first location is connected to the second location.

BRIEF DESCRIPTION OF THE DRAWINGS

For a more complete understanding of the present invention and the advantages thereof, reference is now made to the following description taken in conjunction with the accompanying Drawings in which:

FIG. 1 illustrates a block diagram of the preferred embodiment;

FIG. 2 illustrates the computer components employed in this embodiment;

FIG. 3 illustrates system interactions over a global network;

FIGS. 4a-4e illustrate the various message packets transmitted between the source PC and network servers used in the preferred embodiment;

FIG. 5 is a flowchart depicting operation of the system according to the preferred embodiment;

FIG. 6 illustrates a flowchart of actions taken by the Advertiser Reference Server ("ARS") server;

FIG. 7 illustrates a flowchart of the interactive process between the source computer and ARS;

FIG. 8 illustrates a web browser page receiving the modified URL/advertiser product data according to the preferred embodiment;

FIG. 9 illustrates a simplified block diagram of the disclosed embodiment;

FIG. 10 illustrates a more detailed, simplified block diagram of the embodiment of FIG. 9;

FIG. 11 illustrates a diagrammatic view of a method for performing the routing operation;

FIG. 12 illustrates a block diagram of an alternate embodiment utilizing an optical region in the video image for generating the routing information;

FIG. 13 illustrates a block diagram illustrating the generation of a profile with the disclosed embodiment;

3

FIG. **14** illustrates a flowchart for generating the profile and storing at the ARS;

FIG. **15** illustrates a flowchart for processing the profile information when information is routed to a user;

FIG. **16** illustrates a general block diagram of a disclosed embodiment;

FIG. **17** illustrates the conversion circuit of the wedge interface;

FIG. **18** illustrates a sample message packet transmitted from the user PC to the ARS;

FIG. **19** illustrates a more detailed block diagram of the routing of the message packets between the various nodes;

FIG. **20** illustrates a block diagram of a browser window, according to a disclosed embodiment;

FIG. **21** illustrates a diagrammatic view of information contained in the ARS database;

FIG. **22** illustrates a flowchart of the process of receiving information for the user's perspective;

FIG. **23** illustrates a flowchart according to the ARS; and

FIG. **24** illustrates a flowchart of the process performed at the E-commerce node.

DETAILED DESCRIPTION OF THE INVENTION

Referring now to FIG. **1**, there is illustrated a block diagram of a system for controlling a personal computer ("PC") **112** via an audio tone transmitted over a wireless system utilizing a TV. In the embodiment illustrated in FIG. **1**, there is provided a transmission station **101** and a receive station **117** that are connected via a communication link **108**. The transmission station **101** is comprised of a television program source **104**, which is operable to generate a program in the form of a broadcast signal comprised of video and audio. This is transmitted via conventional techniques along channels in the appropriate frequencies. The program source is input to a mixing device **106**, which mixing device is operable to mix in an audio signal. This audio signal is derived from an audio source **100** which comprises a coded audio signal which is then modulated onto a carrier which is combined with the television program source **104**. This signal combining can be done at the audio level, or it can even be done at the RF level in the form of a different carrier. However, the preferred method is to merely sum the audio signal from the modulator **102** into the audio channel of the program that is generated by the television program source **104**. The output thereof is provided from the mixing device **106** in the form of broadcast signal to an antenna **107**, which transmits the information over the communication link **108** to an antenna **109** on the receive side.

On the receive side of the system, a conventional receiver **110**, such as a television is provided. This television provides a speaker output which provides the user with an audible signal. This is typically associated with the program. However, the receiver **110** in the disclosed embodiment, also provides an audio output jack, this being the type RCA jack. This jack is utilized to provide an audio output signal on a line **113** which is represented by an audio signal **111**. This line **113** provides all of the audio that is received over the communication link **108** to the PC **112** in the audio input port on the PC **112**. However, it should be understood that, although a direct connection is illustrated from the receiver **110** to the PC **112**, there actually could be a microphone pickup at the PC **112** which could pick the audio signal up. In the disclosed embodiment the audio signal generated by the advertiser data input device **100** is audible to the human ear and, therefore, can be heard by the user. Therefore, no special filters are needed to provide this audio to the PC **112**.

The PC **112** is operable to run programs thereon which typically are stored in a program file area **116**. These programs can be any type of programs such as word processing programs, application programs, etc. In the disclosed embodiment, the program that is utilized in the system is what is referred to as a "browser." The PC **112** runs a browser program to facilitate the access of information on the network, for example, a global communication network known as the "Internet" or the World-Wide-Web ("Web"). The browser is a hypertext-linked application used for accessing information. Hypertext is a term used to describe a particular organization of information within a data processing system, and its presentation to a user. It exploits the computer's ability to link together information from a wide variety of sources to provide the user with the ability to explore a particular topic. The traditional style of presentation used in books employs an organization of the information which is imposed upon it by limitations of the medium, namely fixed sized, sequential paper pages. Hypertext systems, however, use a large number of units of text or other types of data such as image information, graphical information, video information, or sound information, which can vary in size. A collection of such units of information is termed a hypertext document, or where the hypertext documents employ information other than text, hypermedia documents. Multimedia communications may use the Hypertext Transfer Protocol ("HTTP"), and files or formatted data may use the Hypertext Markup Language ("HTML"). This formatting language provides for a mingling of text, graphics, sound, video, and hypertext links by "tagging" a text document using HTML. Data encoded using HTML is often referred to as an "HTML document," an "HTML page," or a "home page." These documents and other Internet resources may be accessed across the network by means of a network addressing scheme which uses a locator referred to as a Uniform Resource Locator ("URL"), for example, "http://www.digital.com."

The Internet is one of the most utilized networks for interconnecting distributed computer systems and allows users of these computer systems to exchange data all over the world. Connected to the Internet are many private networks, for example, corporate or commercial networks. Standard protocols, such as the Transport Control Protocol ("TCP") and the Internet Protocol ("IP") provide a convenient method for communicating across these diverse networks. These protocols dictate how data are formatted and communicated. As a characteristic of the Internet, the protocols are layered in an IP stack. At higher levels of the IP stack, such as the application layer (where HTTP is employed), the user information is more readily visible, while at lower levels, such as the network level (where TCP/IP are used), the data can merely be observed as packets or a stream of rapidly moving digital signals. Superimposed on the Internet is a standard protocol interface for accessing Web resources, such as servers, files, Web pages, mail messages, and the like. One way that Web resources can be accessed is by browsers made by Netscape® and Microsoft Internet Explorer®.

Referring again now to FIG. **1**, the user can load this program with the appropriate keystrokes such that a browser window will be displayed on a display **118**. In one embodiment, the user can run the browser program on the PC **112** such that the browser window is displayed on the display **118**. While watching a preferred program, the user can also view display **118**. When an audio signal is received by the receiver **110** and the encoded information is contained therein that was input thereto by the advertiser, the PC **112** will then perform a number of operations. The first operation, according to the disclosed embodiment, is to extract the audio information

within the received audio signal in the form of digital data, and then transmit this digital data to a defined location on the global communication network via a modem connection **114**. This connection will be described hereinbelow. This information will be relayed to a proprietary location and the instructions sent back to the PC **112** as to the location of the advertiser associated with the code, and the PC **112** will then effect a communication link to that location such that the user can view on the display **118** information that the advertiser, by the fact of putting the tone onto the broadcast channel, desires the viewer to view. This information can be in the form of interactive programs, data files, etc. In one example, when an advertisement appears on the television, the tone can be generated and then additional data displayed on the display **118**. Additionally, a streaming video program could be played on the PC received over the network, which streaming video program is actually longer than the advertising segment on the broadcast. Another example would be a sports game that would broadcast the tone in order to allow a user access to information that is not available over the broadcast network, such as additional statistics associated with the sports program, etc.

By utilizing the system described herein with respect to the disclosed embodiment of FIG. **1**, an advertiser is allowed the ability to control a user's PC **112** through the use of tones embedded within a program audio signal. As will be described hereinbelow, the disclosed embodiment utilizes particular routing information stored in the PC **112** which allows the encoded information in the received audio signal to route this information to a desired location on the network and then allow other routing information to be returned to the PC **112** for control thereof to route the PC **112** to the appropriate location associated with that code.

Referring now to FIG. **2**, there is illustrated a computer **204**, similar to computer **112**, connected to display information on display **118**. The computer **204** comprises an internal audio or "sound" card **206** for receiving the transmitted audio signal through receive antenna **109** and receiver **110**. The sound card **206** typically contains analog-to-digital circuitry for converting the analog audio signal into a digital signal. The digital signal may then be more easily manipulated by software programs. The receiver **110** separates the audio signal from the video signal. A special trigger signal located within the transmitted advertiser audio signal triggers proprietary software running on the computer **204** which launches a communication application, in this particular embodiment, the web browser application located on the PC **204**. Coded advertiser information contained within the audio signal is then extracted and appended with the address of a proprietary server located on the communication network. The remote server address is in the form of a URL. This appended data, in addition to other control codes, is inserted directly into the web browser application for automatic routing to the communication network. The web browser running on PC **204**, and communicating to the network through an internal modem **208**, in this embodiment, transmits the advertiser information to the remote server. The remote server cross-references the advertiser product information to the address of the advertiser server located on the network. The address of the advertiser server is routed back through the PC **204** web browser to the advertiser server. The advertiser product information is returned to PC **204** to be presented to the viewer on display **118**. In this particular embodiment, the particular advertiser product information displayed is contained within the advertiser's web page **212**. As mentioned above, the audio signal is audible to the human ear. Therefore the audio signal, as emitted from the TV speakers, may be input to the sound card **206**

via a microphone. Furthermore, the audio signal need not be a real-time broadcast, but may be on video tapes, CDs, DVD, or other media which may be displayed at a later date. With the imminent implementation of high definition digital television, the audio signal output from the TV may also be digital. Therefore, direct input into a sound card for A/D purposes may not be necessary, but alternative interfacing techniques to accommodate digital-to-digital signal formats would apply.

Referring now to FIG. **3**, there is illustrated a source PC **302**, similar to PCs **204** and **112**, connected to a global communication network (GCN) **306** through an interface **304**. In this embodiment, the audio signal **111** is received by PC **302** through its sound card **206**. The audio signal **111** comprises a trigger signal which triggers proprietary software into launching a web browser application residing on the PC **302**. The audio signal **111** also comprises advertiser product information which is extracted and appended with URL information of an Advertiser Reference Server ("ARS") **308**. The ARS **308** is a system disposed on the GCN **306** that is defined as the location to which data in the audio signal **111** is to be routed. As such, data in the audio signal **111** will always be routed to the ARS **308**, since a URL is unique on the GCN **306**. Connected to the ARS **308** is a database **310** of product codes and associated manufacturer URLs. The database **310** undergoes a continual update process which is transparent to the user. As companies sign-on, i.e., subscribe, to this technology, manufacturer and product information is added to the database **310** without interrupting operation of the source PC **302** with frequent updates. When the advertiser server address URL is obtained from the ARS database **310**, it and the request for the particular advertiser product information are automatically routed back through the web browser on PC **302**, over to the respective advertiser server for retrieval of the advertiser product information to the PC **302**. Additionally, although the disclosed invention discusses a global communication network, the system is also applicable to LANs, WANs, and peer-to-peer network configurations. It should be noted that the disclosed architecture is not limited to a single source PC **302**, but may comprise a plurality of source PCs, e.g., PC **300** and PC **303**. Moreover, a plurality of ARS **308** systems and advertiser servers **312** may be implemented, e.g., ARS **314**, and advertiser server A **316**, respectively.

The information transactions, in general, which occur between the networked systems of this embodiment, over the communication network, are the following. The web browser running on source PC **302** transmits a message packet to the ARS **308** over Path "A." The ARS **308** decodes the message packet and performs a cross-reference function with product information extracted from the received message packet to obtain the address of an advertiser server **312**. A new message packet is assembled comprising the advertiser server **312** address, and sent back to the source PC **302** over Path "B." A "handoff" operation is performed whereby the source PC **302** browser simply reroutes the information on to the advertiser server **312** over Path "C," with the appropriate source and destination address appended. The advertiser server **312** receives and decodes the message packet. The request-for-advertiser-product-information is extracted and the advertiser **312** retrieves the requested information from its database for transmission back to the source PC **302** over Path "D." The source PC **302** then processes the information, i.e., for display to the viewer. The optional Path "E" is discussed hereinbelow. It should be noted that the disclosed methods are not limited to only browser communication applications, but may accommodate, with sufficient modifications by one skilled in

the art, other communication applications used to transmit information over the Internet or communication network.

Referring now to FIG. 4a, the message packet 400 sent from the source PC 302 to ARS 308 via Path "A" comprises several fields. One field comprises the URL of the ARS 308 which indicates where the message packet is to be sent. Another field comprises the advertiser product code or other information derived from the audio signal 111, and any additional overhead information required for a given transaction. The product code provides a link to the address of the advertiser server 312, located in the database 310. Yet another field comprises the network address of the source PC 302. In general, network transmissions are effected in packets of information, each packet providing a destination address, a source address, and data. These packets vary depending upon the network transmission protocol utilized for communication. Although the protocols utilized in the disclosed embodiment are of a conventional protocol suite commonly known as TCP/IP, it should be understood that any protocols providing the similar basic functions can be used, with the primary requirement that a browser can forward the routing information to the desired URL in response to keystrokes being input to a PC. However, it should be understood that any protocol can be used, with the primary requirement that a browser can forward the product information to the desired URL in response to keystrokes being input to a PC. Within the context of this disclosure, "message packet" shall refer to and comprise the destination URL, product information, and source address, even though more than a single packet must be transmitted to effect such a transmission.

Upon receipt of the message packet 400 from source PC 302, ARS 308 processes the information in accordance with instructions embedded in the overhead information. The ARS 308 specifically will extract the product code information from the received packet 400 and, once extracted, will then decode this product code information. Once decoded, this information is then compared with data contained within the ARS advertiser database 310 to determine if there is a "hit." If there is no "hit" indicating a match, then information is returned to the browser indicating such. If there is a "hit," a packet 402 is assembled which comprises the address of the source PC 302, and information instructing the source PC 302 as to how to access, directly in a "handoff" operation, another location on the network, that of an advertiser server 312. This type of construction is relatively conventional with browsers such as Netscape® and Microsoft Internet Explorer® and, rather than displaying information from the ARS 308, the source PC 302 can then access the advertiser server 312. The ARS 308 transmits the packet 402 back to source PC 302 over Path "B." Referring now to FIG. 4b, the message packet 402 comprises the address of the source PC 302, the URL of the advertiser server 312 embedded within instructional code, and the URL of the ARS 308.

Upon receipt of the message packet 402 by the source PC 302, the message packet 402 is disassembled to obtain pertinent routing information for assembly of a new message packet 404. The web browser running on source PC 302 is now directed to obtain, over Path "C," the product information relevant to the particular advertiser server 312 location information embedded in message packet 404. Referring now to FIG. 4c, the message packet 404 for this transaction comprises the URL of the advertiser server 312, the request-for-product-information data, and the address of the source PC 302.

Upon receipt of the message packet 404 from source PC 302, advertiser server 312 disassembles the message packet 404 to obtain the request-for-product-information data. The

advertiser server 312 then retrieves the particular product information from its database, and transmits it over Path "D" back to the source PC 302. Referring now to FIG. 4d, the message packet 406 for this particular transaction comprises the address of the source PC 302, the requested information, and the URL of the advertiser server 312.

Optionally, the ARS 308 may make a direct request for product information over Path "E" to advertiser server 312. In this mode, the ARS 308 sends information to the advertiser server 312 instructing it to contact the source PC 302. This, however, is unconventional and requires more complex software control. The message packet 408 for this transaction is illustrated in FIG. 4e, which comprises the URL of the advertiser server 312, the request-for-product-information data, and the address of the source PC 302. Since product information is not being returned to the ARS 308, but directly to the source PC 302, the message packet 408 requires the return address to be that of the source PC 302. The product information is then passed directly to PC 302 over Path "D."

Referring now to FIG. 5, the method for detecting and obtaining product information is as follows. In decision block 500, a proprietary application running resident on a source computer PC 302 (similar to PC 204) monitors the audio input for a special trigger signal. Upon detection of the trigger signal, data following the trigger signal is decoded for further processing, in function block 502. In function block 504, the data is buffered for further manipulation. In decision block 506, a determination is made as to whether the data can be properly authenticated. If not, program flow continues through the "N" signal to function block 520 where the data is discarded. In function block 522, the program then signals for a retransmission of the data. The system then waits for the next trigger signal, in decision block 500. If properly authenticated in decision block 506, program flow continues through the "Y" signal path where the data is then used to launch the web browser application, as indicated in function block 508. In function block 510, the web browser receives the URL data, which is then automatically routed through the computer modem 208 to the network interface 304 and ultimately to the network 306. In function block 514, the ARS 308 responds by returning the URL of advertiser server 312 to the PC 302. In function block 516, the web browser running on the source PC 302, receives the advertiser URL information from the ARS 308, and transmits the URL for the product file to the advertiser server 312. In block 518, the advertiser server 312 responds by sending the product information to the source PC 302 for processing.

The user may obtain the benefits of this architecture by simply downloading the proprietary software over the network. Other methods for obtaining the software are well-known; for example, by CD, diskette, or pre-loaded hard drives.

Referring now to FIG. 6, there is illustrated a flowchart of the process the ARS 308 may undergo when receiving the message packet 400 from the source PC 302. In decision block 600, the ARS 308 checks for the receipt of the message packet 400. If a message packet 400 is not received, program flow moves along the "N" path to continue waiting for the message. If the message packet 400 is received, program flow continues along path "Y" for message processing. Upon receipt of the message packet 400, in function block 602, the ARS 308 decodes the message packet 400. The product code is then extracted independently in function block 604 in preparation for matching the product code with the appropriate advertiser server address located in the database 310. In function block 606, the product code is then used with a lookup table to retrieve the advertiser server 312 URL of the

respective product information contained in the audio signal data. In function block **608**, the ARS **308** then assembles message packet **402** for transmission back to the source PC **302**. Function block **610** indicates the process of sending the message packet **402** back to the source PC **302** over Path "B."

Referring now to FIG. **7**, there is illustrated a flowchart of the interactive processes between the source PC **302** and the advertiser server **312**. In function block **700**, the source PC **302** receives the message packet **402** back from the ARS **308** and begins to decode the packet **402**. In function block **702**, the URL of the advertiser product information is extracted from the message packet **402** and saved for insertion into the message packet **404** to the advertiser server **312**. The message packet **404** is then assembled and sent by the source PC **302** over Path "C" to the advertiser server **312**, in function block **704**. While the source PC **302** waits, in function block **706**, the advertiser server **312** receives the message packet **404** from the source PC **302**, in function block **708**, and disassembles it. The product information location is then extracted from the message packet **404** in function block **710**. The particular product information is retrieved from the advertiser server **312** database for transmission back to the source PC **302**. In function block **712**, the product information is assembled into message packet **406** and then transmitted back to the source PC **302** over Path "D." Returning to the source PC **302** in function block **714**, the advertiser product information contained in the message packet **406** received from the advertiser server **312**, is then extracted and processed in function block **716**.

Referring now to FIG. **8**, after receipt of a trigger signal, a web browser application on a source PC **302** is automatically launched and computer display **800** presents a browser page **802**. Proprietary software running on the source PC **302** processes the audio signal data after being digitized through the sound card **206**. The software appropriately prepares the data for insertion directly into the web browser by extracting the product information code and appending keystroke data to this information. First, a URL page **804** is opened in response to a Ctrl-O command added by the proprietary software as the first character string. Opening URL page **804** automatically positions the cursor in a field **806** where additional keystroke data following the Ctrl-O command will be inserted. After URL page **804** is opened, the hypertext protocol preamble http:// is inserted into the field **806**. Next, URL information associated with the location of the ARS **308** is inserted into field **806**. Following the ARS **308** URL data are the characters /? to allow entry of variables immediately following the /? characters. In this embodiment, the variable following is the product information code received in the audio signal. The product code information also provides the cross-reference information for obtaining the advertiser URL from the ARS database **310**. Next, a carriage return is added to send the URL/product data and close the window **804**. After the message packet **400** is transmitted to the ARS **308** from the source PC **302**, transactions from the ARS **308**, to the source PC **302**, to the advertiser server **312**, and back to the source PC **302**, occur quickly and are transparent to the viewer. At this point, the next information the viewer sees is the product information which was received from the advertiser server **312**.

Referring now to FIG. **9**, there is illustrated a block diagram of a more simplified embodiment. In this embodiment, a video source **902** is provided which is operable to provide an audio output on an audio cable **901** which provides routing information referred to by reference numeral **904**. The routing information **904** is basically information contained within the audio signal. This is an encoded or embedded signal. The important aspect of the routing information **904** is that it is

automatically output in realtime as a function of the broadcast of the video program received over the video source **902**. Therefore, whenever the program is being broadcast in realtime to the user **908**, the routing information **904** will be output whenever the producer of the video desires it to be produced. It should be understood that the box **902** representing the video source could be any type of media that will result in the routing information being output. This could be a cassette player, a DVD player, an audio cassette, a CD ROM or any such media. It is only important that this is a program that the producer develops which the user **908** watches in a continuous or a streaming manner. Embedded within that program, at a desired point selected by the producer, the routing information **904** is output.

The audio information is then routed to a PC **906**, which is similar to the PC **112** in FIG. **1**. A user **908** is interfaced with the PC to receive information thereof, the PC **906** having associated therewith a display (not shown). The PC **906** is interfaced with a network **910**, similar to the network **306** in FIG. **3**. This network **910** has multiple nodes thereon, one of which is the PC **906**, and another of which is represented by a network node **912** which represents remote information. The object of the present embodiment is to access remote information for display to the user **908** by the act of transmitting from the video program in block **902** the routing information **904**. This routing information **904** is utilized to allow the PC **906** which has a network "browser" running thereon to "fetch" the remote information at the node **912** over the network **910** for display to the user **908**. This routing information **904** is in the form of an embedded code within the audio signal, as was described hereinabove.

Referring now to FIG. **10**, there is illustrated a more detailed block diagram of the embodiment of FIG. **9**. In this embodiment, the PC **906** is split up into a couple of nodes, a first PC **1002** and a second PC **1004**. The PC **1002** resides at the node associated with the user **908**, and the PC **1004** resides at another node. The PC **1004** represents the ARS **308** of FIG. **3**. The PC **1004** has a database **1006** associated therewith, which is basically the advertiser database **310**. Therefore, there are three nodes on the network **910** necessary to implement the disclosed embodiment, the PC **1002**, the PC **1004** and the remote information node **912**. The routing information **904** is utilized by the PC **1002** for routing to the PC **1004** to determine the location of the remote information node **912** on the network **910**. This is returned to the PC **1002** and a connection made directly with the remote information node **912** and the information retrieved therefrom to the user **908**. The routing information **904** basically constitutes primary routing information.

Referring now to FIG. **11**, there is illustrated a diagrammatic view of how the network packet is formed for sending the primary routing information to the PC **1004**. In general, the primary routing information occupies a single field which primary routing information is then assembled into a data packet with the secondary routing information for transfer to the network **910**. This is described hereinabove in detail.

Referring now to FIG. **12**, there is illustrated an alternate embodiment to that of FIG. **9**. In this embodiment, the video source **902** has associated therewith an optical region **1202**, which optical region **1202** has disposed therein an embedded video code. This embedded video code could be relatively complex or as simple as a grid of dark and white regions, each region in the grid able to have a dark color for a logic "1" or a white region for a logic "0." This will allow a digital value to be disposed within the optical region **1202**. A sensor **1204** can then be provided for sensing this video code. In the example above, this would merely require an array of optical

detectors, one for each region in the grid to determine whether this is a logic "1" or a logic "0" state. One of the sensed video is then output to the PC **906** for processing thereof to determine the information contained therein, which information contained therein constitutes the primary routing information **904**. Thereafter, it is processed as described hereinabove with reference to FIG. **9**.

Referring now to FIG. **13**, there is illustrated a block diagram for an embodiment wherein a user's profile can be forwarded to the original subscriber or manufacturer. The PC **906** has associated therewith a profile database **1302**, which profile database **1302** is operable to store a profile of the user **908**. This profile is created when the program, after initial installation, requests profile information to be input in order to activate the program. In addition to the profile, there is also a unique ID that is provided to the user **908** in association with the browser program that runs on the PC **906**. This is stored in a storage location represented by a block **1304**. This ID **1304** is accessible by a remote location as a "cookie" which is information that is stored in the PC **906** in an accessible location, which accessible location is actually accessible by the remote program running on a remote node.

The ARS **308**, which basically constitutes the PC **1004** of FIG. **10**, is operable to have associated therewith a profile database **1308**, which profile database **1308** is operable to store profiles for all of the users. The profile database **1308** is a combination of the stored information in profile database **1302** for all of the PCs **906** that are attachable to the system. This is to be distinguished from information stored in the database **310** of the ARS **308**, the advertiser's database, which contains intermediate destination tables. When the routing information in the primary routing information **904** is forwarded to the ARS **308** and extracted from the original data packet, the lookup procedure described hereinabove can then be performed to determine where this information is to be routed. The profile database **1302** is then utilized for each transaction, wherein each transaction in the form of the routing information received from the primary routing information **904** is compared to the destination tables of database **310** to determine what manufacturer is associated therewith. The associated ID **1304** that is transmitted along with the routing information in primary routing information **904** is then compared with the profile database **1308** to determine if a profile associated therewith is available. This information is stored in a transaction database **1310** such that, at a later time, for each routing code received in the form of the information in primary routing information **904**, there will associated therewith the IDs **1304** of each of the PCs **906**. The associated profiles in database **1308**, which are stored in association with IDs **1304**, can then be assembled and transmitted to a subscriber as referenced by a subscriber node **1312** on the network **910**. The ARS **308** can do this in two modes, a realtime mode or a non-realtime mode. In a realtime mode, each time a PC **906** accesses the advertiser database **310**, that user's profile information is uploaded to the subscriber node **1312**. At the same time, billing information is generated for that subscriber **1312** which is stored in a billing database **1316**. Therefore, the ARS **308** has the ability to inform the subscriber **1312** of each transaction, bill for those transactions, and also provide to the subscriber **1312** profile information regarding who is accessing the particular product advertisement having associated therewith the routing information field **904** for a particular routing code as described hereinabove. This information, once assembled, can then be transmitted to the subscriber **1312** and also be reflected in billing information and stored in the billing information database **1316**.

Referring now to FIG. **14**, there is illustrated a flowchart depicting the operation for storing the profile for the user. The program is initiated in a block **1402** and then proceeds to a function block **1404**, wherein the system will prompt for the profile upon initiation of the system. This initiation is a function that is set to activate whenever the user initially loads the software that he or she is provided. The purpose for this is to create, in addition to the setup information, a user profile. Once the user is prompted for this, then the program will flow to a decision block **1406** to determine whether the user provides basic or detailed information. This is selectable by the user. If selecting basic, the program will flow to a function block **1408** wherein the user will enter basic information such as name and serial number and possibly an address. However, to provide some incentive to the user to enter more information, the original prompt in function block **1404** would have offers for such things as coupons, discounts, etc., if the user will enter additional information. If the user selects this option, the program flows from the decision block **1406** to a function block **1410**. In the function block **1410**, the user is prompted to enter specific information such as job, income level, general family history, demographic information and more. There can be any amount of information collected in this particular function block.

Once all of the information is collected, in either the basic mode or the more specific mode, the program will then flow to a function block **1412** where this information is stored locally. The program then flows to a decision block **1414** to then go on-line to the host or the ARS **308**. In general, the user is prompted to determine whether he or she wants to send this information to the host at the present time or to send it later. If he or she selects the "later" option, the program will flow to a function block **1415** to prompt the user at a later time to send the information. In the disclosed embodiment, the user will not be able to utilize the software until the profile information is sent to the host. Therefore, the user may have to activate this at a later time in order to connect with the host.

If the user has selected the option to upload the profile information to the host, the program will flow to the function block **1416** to initiate the connect process and then to a decision block **1418** to determine if the connection has been made. If not, the program will flow along a "N" path to decision block **1420** which will timeout to an error block **1422** or back to the input of the connect decision block **1418**. The program, once connected, will then flow along a "Y" path from decision block **1418** to a function block **1428** to send the profile information with the ID of the computer or user to the host. The ID is basically, as described hereinabove, a "cookie" in the computer which is accessed by the program when transmitting to the host. The program will then flow to a function block **1430** to activate the program such that it, at later time, can operate without requiring all of the setup information. In general, all of the operation of this flowchart is performed with a "wizard," which steps the user through the setup process. Once complete, the program will flow to a Done block **1432**.

Referring now to FIG. **15**, there is illustrated a flowchart depicting the operation of the host when receiving a transaction. The program is initiated at a Start block **1502** and then proceeds to decision block **1504**, wherein it is determined whether the system has received a routing request, i.e., the routing information **904** in the form of a tone, etc., embedded in the audio signal, as described hereinabove with respect to FIG. **9**. The program will loop back around to the input of decision block **1504** until the routing request has been received. At this time, the program will flow along the "Y" path to a function block **1506** to receive the primary routing

information and the user ID. Essentially, this primary routing information is extracted from the audio tone, in addition to the user ID. The program then flows to a function block **1508** to look up the manufacturer URL that corresponds to the received primary routing information and then return the necessary command information to the originating PC **112** in order to allow that PC **112** to connect to the destination associated with the primary routing information. Thereafter, the program will flow to a function block **1510** to update the transaction database **1310** for the current transaction. In general, the routing information **904** will be stored as a single field with the associated IDs. The profile database **1308**, as described hereinabove, has associated therewith detailed profiles of each user on the system that has activated their software in association with their ID. Since the ID was sent in association with the routing information, what is stored in the transaction database **1310** is the routing code, in association with all of the IDs transmitted to the system in association with that particular routing code. Once this transaction database **1310** has been updated, as described hereinabove, the transactions can be transferred back to the subscriber at node **312** with the detailed profile information from the profile database **1308**.

The profile information can be transmitted back to the subscriber or manufacturer at the node **312** in realtime or non-realtime. A decision block **1512** is provided for this, which determines if the delivery is realtime. If realtime, the program will flow along a "Y" path to a function block **1514** wherein the information will be immediately forwarded to the manufacturer or subscriber. The program will then flow to a function block **1516** wherein the billing for that particular manufacturer or subscriber will be updated in the billing database **1316**. The program will then flow into an End block **1518**. If it was non-realtime, the program moves along the "N" path to a function block **1520** wherein it is set for a later delivery and it is accrued in the transaction database **1310**. In any event, the transaction database **1310** will accrue all information associated with a particular routing code.

With a realtime transaction, it is possible for a manufacturer to place an advertisement in a magazine or to place a product on a shelf at a particular time. The manufacturer can thereafter monitor the times when either the advertisements or the products are purchased. Of course, they must be scanned into a computer which will provide some delay. However, the manufacturer can gain a very current view of how a product is moving. For example, if a cola manufacturer were to provide a promotional advertisement on, for example, television, indicating that a new cola was going to be placed on the shelf and that the first **1000** purchasers, for example, scanning their code into the network would receive some benefit, such as a chance to win a trip to some famous resort in Florida or some other incentive, the manufacturer would have a very good idea as to how well the advertisement was received. Further, the advertiser would know where the receptive markets were. If this advertiser, for example, had placed the television advertisement in ten cities and received overwhelming response from one city, but very poor response from another city, he would then have some inclination to believe that either the one poor response city was not a good market or that the advertising medium he had chosen was very poor. Since the advertiser can obtain a relatively instant response and also content with that response as to the demographics of the responder, very important information can be obtained in a relatively short time.

It should be noted that the disclosed embodiment is not limited to a single source PC **302**, but may encompass a large number of source computers connected over a global communication network. Additionally, the embodiment is not limited to a single ARS **308** or a single advertiser server **312**, but may include a plurality of ARS and advertiser systems, indicated by the addition of ARS **314** and advertiser server A **316**, respectively. It should also be noted that this embodiment is not limited only to global communication networks, but also may be used with LAN, WAN, and peer-to-peer configurations.

It should also be noted that the disclosed embodiment is not limited to a personal computer, but is also applicable to, for example, a Network Computer ("NetPC"), a scaled-down version of the PC, or any system which accommodates user interaction and interfaces to information resources.

One typical application of the above noted technique is for providing a triggering event during a program, such as a sport event. In a first example, this may be generated by an advertiser. One could imagine that, due to the cost of advertisements in a high profile sports program, there is a desire to utilize this time wisely. If, for example, an advertiser contracted for 15 seconds worth of advertising time, they could insert within their program a tone containing the routing information. This routing information can then be output to the user's PC **302**, which will cause the user's PC **302** to, via the network, obtain information from a remote location typically controlled by the advertiser. This could be in the form of an advertisement of a length longer than that contracted for. Further, this could be an interactive type of advertisement. An important aspect to the type of interaction between the actual broadcast program with the embedded routing information and the manufacturer's site is the fact that there is provided information as to the user's PC **302** and a profile of the user themselves. Therefore, an advertiser can actually gain realtime information as to the number of individuals that are watching their particular advertisement and also information as to the background of those individuals, profile information, etc. This can be a very valuable asset to an advertiser.

In another example, the producer of the program, whether it be an on-air program, a program embedded in a video tape, CD-ROM, DVD, or a cassette, can allow the user to automatically access additional information that is not displayed on the screen. For example, in a sporting event, various statistics can be provided to the user from a remote location, merely by the viewer watching the program. When these statistics are provided, the advertiser can be provided with profile information and background information regarding the user. This can be important when, for example, the user may record a sports program. If the manufacturer sees that this program routing code is being output from some device at a time later than the actual broadcast itself, this allows the advertisers to actually see that their program is still being used and also what type of individual is using it. Alternatively, the broadcaster could determine the same and actually bill the advertiser an additional sum for a later broadcast. This is all due to the fact that the routing information automatically, through a PC and a network, will provide an indication to the advertiser the time at which the actual information was broadcast.

The different type of medium that can be utilized with the above embodiment are such things as advertisements, which are discussed hereinabove, contests, games, news programs, education, coupon promotional programs, demonstration media (demos), photographs, all of which can be broadcast on a private site or a public site. This all will provide the ability to allow realtime interface with the network and the remote location for obtaining the routed information and also allow for realtime billing and accounting.

Referring now to FIG. **16**, there is illustrated a general block diagram of a disclosed embodiment. A bar code scan-

ning wand **1600** is provided by a wand distributor to customers and is associated with that distributor via a wand ID stored therein. The wand **1600** is either sold or freely distributed to customers for use with their personal computing systems. Since more and more products are being sold using bar codes, it can be appreciated that a user having the wand **1600** can scan bar codes of a multitude of products in order to obtain more information. Information about these products can be made immediately available to the user from the manufacturer for presentation by the user's computer **302**. Beyond simply displaying information about the product in which the user is interested, the wand distributor may include additional advertising information for display to the user such as information about other promotions or products provided or sold by the wand distributor. Similarly, advertisers may provide catalogs of advertisements or information in newspapers or periodicals where the user simply scans the bar code associated with the advertisement using the wand **1600** to obtain further information. There is provided a paper source **1602** having contained thereon an advertisement **1604** and an associated bar code **1606**. (Note that the disclosed concept is not limited to scanning of bar codes **1606** from paper sources **1602**, but is also operable to scan a bar code **1606** on the product itself. Also, the wand **1600** can be any type of device that will scan any type of image having information encoded therein.)

After obtaining the wand **1600** from the wand distributor, the user connects the wand **1600** to their PC **302**. During a scanning operation, wand **1600** reads bar code data **1606** and the wand ID into a "wedge" interface **1608** for conversion into keyboard data, which keyboard data is passed therefrom into the keyboard input port of PC **302**. The importance of the wand ID will be discussed in more detail hereinbelow.

The wedge interface **1608** is simply an interface box containing circuitry that accommodates inputs from both the scanning wand **1600** and a computer keyboard **1610**. This merely allows the information scanned by the wand **1600** to be input into the PC **302**. In the disclosed embodiment, the wedge interface **1608** will convert any information. The data output from the wand **1600** is passed into the wedge interface **1608** for conversion into keyboard data which is readily recognizable by the PC **302**. Therefore, the wand **1600** is not required to be connected to a separate port on the PC **302**. This data is recognized as a sequence of keystrokes. However, the output of the wand **1600** can be input in any manner compatible with the PC **302**. When not receiving scanner data, the wedge interface **1608** simply acts as a pass-through device for keyboard data from the keyboard **1610**. In any case, the information is ultimately processed by a processor in the PC **302** and can be presented to the user on a display **1612**. The wedge interface **1608** is operable to provide a decoding function for the bar code **1606** and conversion thereof to keystroke input data.

In operation, the product code of a product is provided in the form of a bar code **1606**. This bar code **1606** is the "link" to a product. The disclosed embodiment is operable to connect that product information contained in the bar code **1606** with a web page of the manufacturer of that product by utilizing the bar code **1606** as the product "identifier." The program operating on the PC **302** provides routing information to the ARS **308** after launching the browser on the PC **302** and connecting to the ARS **308** over the GCN **306**, which ARS **308** then performs the necessary steps to cause the browser to connect to the manufacturer web site, while also providing for an accounting step, as will be described in more detail hereinbelow.

The bar code **1606** by itself is incompatible with any kind of network for the purposes of communication therewith. It is primarily provided for a retail-type setting. Therefore, the information contained in the bar code **1606**, by itself, does not allow for anything other than identification of a product, assuming that one has a database **1614** containing information as to a correlation between the product and the bar code **1606**.

The wedge interface **1608** is operable to decode the bar code **1606** to extract the encoded information therein, and append to that decoded bar code information relating to an ID for the wand **1600**. This information is then forwarded to the ARS **308** by the resident program in the PC **302**. This is facilitated by intermediate routing information stored in the program indicating to which node on the GCN **306** the scanned bar code information is to be sent, i.e., to the ARS **308**. It is important to note that the information in the bar code **1606** must be converted from its optical image to numerical values which are then ultimately input to the keyboard input port of PC **302** and converted into data compatible with communication software residing on the PC **302** (in this case, HTML language for insertion into a browser program). When the scanned information is input to the PC **302**, the resident program launches the browser program and then assembles a communication packet comprised of the URL of the ARS **308**, the wand ID and the user ID. If another type of communications program were utilized, then it would have to be converted into language compatible with that program. Of course, a user could actually key in the information on the bar code **102** and then append the appropriate intermediate routing information thereafter. As will be described hereinbelow, the intermediate routing information appended thereto is the URL of the ARS **308** disposed on the GCN **306**.

As part of the configuration for using the wand **1600**, the PC **302** hosts wand software which is operable to interpret data transmitted from the wand **1600**, and to create a message packet having the scanned product information and wand ID, routing information, and a user ID which identifies the user location of the wand **1600**. The wand software loads at bootup of the PC **302** and runs in the background. In response to receiving a scanned bar code **1606**, the wedge interface **1608** outputs a keystroke code (e.g., ALT-F10) to bring the wand program into the foreground for interaction by the operating system. The wand program then inserts the necessary information into the browser program. The message packet is then transmitted to interface **304** across the global communication network **306** to the ARS **308**. The ARS **308** interrogates the message packet and performs a lookup function using the ARS database **310**. If a match is found between particular parameters of the message packet, a return message packet is sent back to the PC **302** for processing.

The wand program running on PC **302** functions to partition the browser window displayed to the user into several individual areas. This is for the purpose of preparing to present to the user selected information in each of the individual areas (also called "framing"). The selected information comprises the product information which the user requested by scanning the bar code **1606** using the wand **1600**, information about the wand distributor which establishes the identity of the company associated with that particular wand **1600**, and at least one or more other frames which may be advertisements related to other products that the wand distributor sells. Note that the advertisements displayed by the wand distributor may be related to the product of interest or totally unrelated. For example, if a user scans the bar code **1606** of a soda from Company A, the wand distributor may generate an advertisement of a new soft drink being

marketed by Company A, that it sells. On the other hand, the wand distributor may also structure the display of information to the user such that a user requesting product information of a Product X may get the requested information of Product X along with advertisements for a competing item Product Y. Essentially, the wand distributor is free to generate any advertisement to the user in response to the user requesting product information.

The return message packet transmitted from the ARS **308** to the PC **302** is then transmitted back across the GCN **306** to the advertiser server **312**. The advertiser server **312** restructures the message packet and appends the particular product information for transmission back to the PC **302**. Upon receiving the particular advertiser information from advertiser server **312**, the PC **302** then retransmits a message to the wand distributor site **1616** and E-commerce site **1618** to obtain the information that needs to be framed in the browser window displayed to the user.

Therefore, the wand **1600** is associated with the wand distributor by way of a wand ID such that scanning a product bar code **1606** in order to obtain information about that particular product generates one or more responses from one or more remote sites disposed on the GCN **306**. Stored in the wand **1600** is the wand ID which establishes its relationship to the wand distributor. Proprietary wand software running on the PC **302** operates to decode scanned bar code information and the wand ID received from the wand **1600** and wedge interface **1608**, and also provides a unique user ID for establishing the location of the user of the wand **1600**. The wand software also assembles message packets and works in conjunction with the on-board communication software (e.g., a browser) to automatically route the message packets across the GCN **306** such that the one or more remote sites disposed on the GCN **306** return information to be framed for presentation to the user.

Referring now to FIG. **17**, there is illustrated a conversion circuit of the wedge interface. A microcontroller **1700** provides conversion of the data from the wand **1600** and controls interfacing of the keyboard **1610** and wand **1600** with the PC **302**. The microcontroller **1700** has contained therein a memory **1702** or it can have external memory. There are provided a plurality of wand interfaces **1704** to the wand **1600**, a plurality of PC interfaces **1706** to the PC **302**, and plurality of keyboard interfaces **1708** to the keyboard **1610**. In general, the wand interfaces **1704** comprise a serial data line, a ground line, and a power line. Similarly, the keyboard interfaces **1708** comprise a serial data line, a ground line, a clock line, and a power line. The PC **302** provides a clock line, a power line, a serial data, and a ground line for input to the microcontroller **1700**. The microcontroller **1700** is operable to receive signals from the keyboard **1610** and transfer the signals to the PC **302** as keyboard signals. Operation with the keyboard **1610** is essentially a "pass-through" procedure. Data output from the keyboard **1610** is already in keyboard format, and therefore requires no conversion by the wedge interface **1608**. With respect to the wand **1600**, the serial data is not compatible with a keyboard **1610** and, therefore, it must be converted into a keyboard format in order to allow input thereof to the keyboard input of the PC **302**.

The microcontroller **1700** performs this function after decoding this bar code information, and conversion of this bar code information into an appropriate stream of data which is comprised of the bar code information and the appended URL. This appended URL will be pre-stored in the memory **1702** and is programmable at the time of manufacture. It is noted that the memory **1702** is illustrated as being contained within the microcontroller **1702** to provide a single chip solu-

tion. However, this could be external memory that is accessible by the microcontroller **1702**. Therefore, the microcontroller **1700** provides an interface between the wand **1600** and the keyboard **1610** to the PC **302** which allows the wand **1600** to receive coded information and convert it to keyboard strokes or, alternatively, to merely pass-through the keystrokes from the keyboard **1610**. Therefore, the user need not install any type of plug-in circuit board into the motherboard of the PC **302** in order to provide an interface to the wand **1600**; rather, the user need only utilize the already available keyboard port in order to input the appropriate data into the system.

In this particular disclosed embodiment, the microcontroller **1700** comprises a PIC 16C73 microcontroller by Microchip Technologies™. The PIC16C73 device is a low cost CMOS 8-bit microcontroller with an integrated analog-to-digital converter. The PIC16C73 device, as illustrated in the disclosed embodiment, has 192 bytes of RAM and 4 k×4 of EPROM memory. The microcontroller **1700** can accommodate asynchronous or synchronous inputs from input devices connected to it. In this disclosed embodiment, communication to the keyboard **1610** is synchronous while it is asynchronous when communicating with wand **1600**.

It should be noted that, although in this particular embodiment bar code information of the bar code **1606** is input into the keyboard input port of the PC **302**, disclosed methods may also be advantageously utilized with high speed port architectures such as Universal Serial Bus ("USB") and IEEE 1394.

Bar codes are structured to be read in either direction. Timing considerations need to be addressed because of the variety of individuals scanning the bar code introduce a wide variety of scan rates. Bar codes use bars of varying widths. The presence of a black bar generates a positive pulse, and the absence of a black bar generates no pulse. Each character of a conventional bar code has associated therewith seven pulses or bars. Depending on the width of the bars, the time between pulses varies. In this disclosed embodiment, the interface circuitry **1608** performs a "running" calculation of the scan time based upon the rising edge of the pulses commencing with the leader or header information. The minimum and maximum scans times are calculated continuously in software with the interface **1608** during the scanning process to ensure a successful scan by the user.

Referring now to FIG. **18**, there is illustrated a sample message packet transmitted from the user's PC **302** to the ARS **308**. The message packet **1800** comprises a number of bits of information including the bar code information **1802** obtained from the user scanning the bar code **1606** with the wand **1600**; the wand ID **1804** which is embedded in a memory in the wand **1600** and identifies it with a particular wand distributor; and a user ID **1806** which is derived from the software running on the PC **302** and which identifies uniquely with the user location. Note that the message packet includes other necessary information for the proper transmission for point to point.

Referring now to FIG. **19**, there is illustrated a more detailed block diagram of the routing of the message packets in order to present the framed information to the user. As is mentioned hereinabove, when the user scans a bar code **1606** using the wand **1600**, a wand program running on the user PC **302** is operable to interpret the information output by the wand **1600** and generate a message packet for transmission over the GCN **306**. The wand program assembles the message packet such that it is directed to the ARS **308** disposed on the GCN **306**. The message packet contains several pieces of information including the wand ID **1804** which links it to the

wand distributor, the user ID **1806** which identifies the particular user using the wand **1600**, and bar code information **1802** describing a particular product of interest to the user. This message from the PC **302** is transmitted over a path **1900** to the ARS **308** where the ARS database **310** is accessed to cross reference the ID information **1804** and bar code information **1802** to a particular advertiser and wand distributor. The ARS **308** returns a message packet over a path **1902** to the user PC **302** which contains routing information as to the location of various other sites disposed on the GCN **306**, for example, the advertiser server **312** and wand distributor site **1616**.

It can be appreciated that other information can also be provided by the ARS **308** which more closely targets the particular user of the wand **1600**. For example, if it is known that a particular wand **1600** is sold in a certain geographic area, this information can be useful in targeting the particular user with certain advertising information relevant to that geographic area. In any case, the information returned from the ARS **308** over path **1902** provides enough information for the wand program running on the user PC **302** to identify a number of other sites disposed on the GCN **306**. The user PC **302** then processes the return message packet and routes another message packet over a path **1904** to the advertiser server **312**. The advertiser server **312** then returns product information of the particular product in which the user was interested back to the user PC **302** over a path **1906**. Similarly, the user PC **302** routes information (e.g., the URL of the wand distributor site and the user profile) to the wand distributor site **1616** over a path **1908** in order to obtain information back over a path **1910** for framing any banners which identify the wand distributor. Additionally, the user PC **302** forwards a message packet to the E-commerce site **1618** over a path **1912** in order to return information regarding any particular advertisements the wand distributor wants to display to the user. The advertisements are returned to the PC **302** over a path **1914**.

Referring now to FIG. **20**, there is illustrated a block diagram of a browser window according to the disclosed embodiment. The browser window **2000** is partitioned into a plurality of areas for framing specific information. A bar code area **2002** displays that product information in which the user was interested; a wand-specific area **2004** displays information about the wand distributor; and an E-commerce area **2006** displays advertising information that the wand distributor selects for display according to this particular user and wand **1600**. As mentioned hereinabove, a program operable to process scanned bar code information with the unique wand **1600** develops the browser window by partitioning it into specific areas for the framing of information. Therefore, information returned from the E-commerce site **1608** is passed through the GCN **306** to the particular E-commerce frame **2006**. Similarly, information about the particular product of interest is returned from the advertiser site **312** across the GCN **306** to the particular bar code specific area **2002**. Information placed in the wand specific area **2004** is information about the wand distributor which is returned from the wand distributor site **1616** across GCN **306**.

Referring now to FIG. **21**, there is illustrated a structure of information contained in the ARS database. The ARS database **310** contains a variety of information required to properly interrogate and assemble packets for obtaining information from the various sites disposed on the GCN **306**. The ARS database **310** has a database structure **2100** which contains addresses for the web sites containing the product information requested by the user when scanning the bar code **1606** with the wand **1600**. Under a product heading **2102** are

listed the particular bar codes and associated routing information for addressing the respective server location. For example, the ARS server **308** may contain any number of advertisers having unique URL addresses associated therewith. Therefore, the bar code **1606** of a particular product is associated with a unique URL address which routes any request for information of that product to that particular advertiser's site. Also part of the ARS database structure **2000** is a heading of wand **2104** under which is the wand ID **1804** and the distributor associated with that wand ID **1804**.

It can be appreciated that there may be a number of distributors using the disclosed architecture such that each distributor has an ID embedded in the wand which uniquely identifies that wand **1600** with the particular distributor. Therefore, the unique wand ID **1804** needs to be listed with the respective distributors of that wand **1600** in order to process the information that needs to be framed and displayed to that particular user. Another heading under the ARS database structure **2100** is a user heading **2106** which contains profile information associated with that particular user ID **1806**. As mentioned hereinabove, the user ID **1806** is obtained via the wand software running on the PC **302** and upon installation or subsequent configuration may request that the user input certain profile information which may be used to target that particular user with products and services which identify with that user profile. The ARS database structure **2100** also contains an E-commerce heading **2108** which contains information related to the bar code **1606** and an advertisement that may be triggered by the request for that information. For example, any bar code **1606** associated with a paper source **1602** can be associated with the specific information in the ARS database **310**. A user wishing to obtain information about a specific soft drink may, in fact, trigger an advertising response of a competitor product. Similarly, the user interested in information about that particular soft drink may also trigger information which is relevant to that particular product or a product which may normally be served in conjunction with that soft drink. Furthermore, if the user profile indicates that this individual has significant interest in finance or insurance, the request for information regarding this particular bar coded product may trigger advertisement from an E-commerce server **1618** related to information about finance and insurance. It should be noted that the information described as contained within the ARS database structure **2100** is not limited to what has been described, but may comprise any number of pieces of information used to present desired information to the computer display of the user.

Referring now to FIG. **22**, there is illustrated a flowchart of the process of receiving information from the user's perspective, and according to the disclosed embodiment. The wand software running on the user's PC **302** runs in the background until activated by output from the wand **1600**. Therefore, flow moves to a decision block **2200** where if a scanned input does not occur, flow moves out the "N" path and loops back to the input of decision block **2200**. On the other hand, if scanned input information is received, flow moves out the "Y" path to a function block **2202** where the wand software assembles a message packet containing the bar code information, the wand ID **1804** and the ARS **308** URL address. Additionally, the browser is launched in which this information is placed for transmission to the ARS **308**. Flow then moves to a function block **2204** where the browser is partitioned into any number of areas in which information is displayed when obtained from the wand distributor site **1616**, the E-commerce site **1618**, and the advertiser server **312**. It should be known that although three frames are shown in the particular window **2000** of this embodiment, the number of frames

displayed in the window **2000** is limited only by the available real estate of the window **2000** area itself.

After the wand software partitions the browser window into one or more frames in preparation of receipt of return information, flow moves to a decision block **2206** where the computer waits for information to be returned from the various sites disposed on the GCN **306**. If information is not returned, flow moves out the "N" path and simply loops back to the input to continue monitoring for receipt of the information. If information has been received, flow moves out the "Y" path to a function block **2208** where routing information for each frame (or partitioned area of the window **2000**) is inserted into one or more packets for transmission to the various sites. The various sites then return the requested information back to the PC **302**, as indicated in function block **2210**. Flow is then to a function block **2212** where the proprietary software working in conjunction with the hosted browser places the returned information into the respective frames of the window. The user, viewing the display at PC **302**, then perceives a variety of information, one of which is the particular product information which he or she requested, in addition to wand distributor information, and possibly other advertisements based upon the user's profile.

Referring now to FIG. **23**, there is illustrated a flowchart of the process according to the ARS. The ARS **308** is operable to decode and process messages received from the GCN **306**. Therefore, flow is to a decision block **2300** where, if bar code information is not received, flow is out the "N" path with loop-back to its input. If bar code information has been received, flow is to a function block **2302** where a matching process occurs to link the bar-coded product information to its respective manufacturer. The ARS database **310** also associates the URL address of the manufacturer's server. When a match is found, the ARS **308** begins to assemble a message packet of information for transmission back to the PC **302**, as indicated in function block **2304**. The message packet contains the product information and the URL address of the manufacturer's website. Flow then moves to a decision block **2306** where the wand ID **1804** is compared with the list of wand IDs issued by the particular wand distributor. If the wand ID **1804** is validated, flow moves out the "Y" path to a function block **2308** where the message packet is appended with the wand ID **1804** and distributor routing address. Flow then moves to a decision block **2310** where the ARS **308** determines if any E-commerce information is to be associated with a particular wand ID **1804**. If so, flow is out the "Y" path to a function block **2312** where the message packet is appended with the E-commerce routing string. The E-commerce routing string provides addressing for the E-commerce server **1618**. Flow then moves to a function block **2314** where all message packets are returned back to the PC **302** for processing.

Referring back to decision block **2306**, if the wand ID **1804** is determined to be invalid, flow moves out the "N" path and jumps forward to the input of decision block **2314**, since the lack of a wand ID **1804** interrupts the link to any advertising provided by the E-commerce server **1618**. At this point, the only information provided is the link to the advertiser server **312** for return of product information. Referring now to decision block **2310**, if no E-commerce information is available, flow moves out the "N" path and jumps forward to the input of function block **2314** where the message packet back to the PC **302** contains only the URL of the advertiser server **312**, the bar code information, the distributor server **1616** address and wand ID **1804** information.

Referring now to FIG. **24**, there is illustrated a flowchart of the process performed at the E-commerce site. The E-com-

merce server **1618** receives the message packet from the user PC **302**, as indicated in function block **2400**, and decodes the packet to perform a match with the bar coded information. Moving on to a decision block **2402**, if the match is unsuccessful, flow is out the "N" path to a function block **2404** where the match is rejected. A message may be returned to indicate that a problem occurred and the user may need to re-scan the product bar code **1606**. If a successful match occurs, flow moves out the "Y" path to a function block **2406** where the wand ID **1804** is matched with the bar code product information. The bar coded information may be distributed to customers over a large geographic area. However, the wand **1606** may be coded for certain geographic areas. For example, a wand **1600** having an XXX ID may be restricted for sale in the Southwestern United States while a wand **1600** having a YYY ID may be sold only in the Northeast. In this way, geographic areas may be targeted with advertising more appealing to that particular area. Advertising returned to the user PC **302** may be focused further by obtaining a user profile when the software or wand **1600** are installed. In this way, advertising may be focused based upon the user profile. Therefore, flow moves to a function block **2408** to lookup the E-commerce action based upon the wand ID **1804** and the bar code information. Flow moves to a function block **2410** to assemble all the information into a packet for return to the user PC **302**. The product information and/or user profile information may be returned. Flow is then to a function block **2412** where the message packet is transmitted.

Although the preferred embodiment has been described in detail, it should be understood that various changes, substitutions and alterations can be made therein without departing from the spirit and scope of the invention as defined by the appended claims.

What is claimed is:

1. A method for interconnecting a first location on a global communication network with a second location thereon, wherein the first location has associated therewith an input device, the input device having associated therewith a unique input device ID that is permanently associated with the input device and independent of the first location, comprising the steps of:

   receiving at the first location a representation of a unique code provided by the input device, which representation of the unique code represents a unique value as an output received from the input device;

   associating the unique value with the unique input device ID in a message packet as a data content portion thereof, such that the unique input device ID is associated with the data content portion of the message packet for transmission over the network and wherein the second location has a predetermined association with the combination of the unique value and the unique input device ID, such predetermined association associates the second location with both the unique input device ID and the unique value; and

   in response to the step of receiving and the step of associating, connecting the first location to the second location.

2. The method of claim **1**, wherein the step of connecting to the second location comprises:

   in response to the step of receiving and the step of associating, accessing a database having stored therein a plurality of unique values, each associated with routing information over the global communication network to one of the plurality of second locations;

   comparing the output unique value with the stored unique values in the database; and

US 8,069,098 B2

23

if a match exists between the output unique value and any of the stored unique values:

retrieving from the database the associated routing information to the second location, and

connecting the first location to the second location on the global communication network in accordance with the retrieved routing information.

3. The method of claim **1**, wherein the unique value comprises a binary value.

4. The method of claim **1**, wherein the unique code comprises a universal product code (UPC) as associated with a product indicating information regarding the product for use in commercial transactions associated with that product.

5. The method of claim **2**, wherein the step of accessing the database comprises the steps of:

accessing a remote location on the global communication network at an intermediate node thereon;

forwarding the unique value and unique input device ID to the intermediate node;

wherein the database is disposed at the intermediate node; and

retrieving the associated routing information from the database in the event of a positive match and forwarding the retrieved routing information back to the first location and connecting the first location to the second location in accordance with the retrieved information.

6. The method of claim **2**, wherein the second location represents product information associated with a product.

7. The method of claim **1**, further comprising:

receiving, at the first location, information from the second location in response to connecting the first location to the second location.

8. The method of claim **7**, further comprising:

presenting the information received from the second location to a user.

9. The method of claim **8**, wherein the step of presenting comprises displaying the information received from the second location via a display at the first location.

10. The method of claim **1**, wherein the step of connecting the first location to the second location is performed using a browser program.

11. An apparatus for interconnecting a first location on a global communication network with a second location thereon, the apparatus comprising:

an input device having associated therewith a unique input device ID that is permanently associated with the input device and independent of the first location, the input device configured to provide a representation of a unique code which represents a unique value;

a processor configured to:

receive at the first location the representation of a unique code provided by the input device as an output received from the input device;

associate the unique value with the unique input device ID in a message packet as a data content portion thereof, such that the unique input device ID is associated with the data content portion of the message packet for transmission over the network and wherein the second location has a predetermined association with the combination of the unique value and the

24

unique input device ID, such predetermined association associates the second location with both the unique input device ID and the unique value; and

in response to the receiving and associating, connect the first location to the second location.

12. The apparatus of claim **11**, wherein the processor is further configured to:

in response to the receiving and the associating, access a database having stored therein a plurality of unique values, each associated with routing information over the global communication network to one of the plurality of second locations;

compare the output unique value with the stored unique values in the database; and

if a match exists between the output unique value and any of the stored unique values:

retrieve from the database the associated routing information to the second location, and

connect the first location to the second location on the global communication network in accordance with the retrieved routing information.

13. The apparatus of claim **11**, wherein the unique value comprises a binary value.

14. The apparatus of claim **11**, wherein the unique code comprises a universal product code (UPC) as associated with a product indicating information regarding the product for use in commercial transactions associated with that product.

15. The apparatus of claim **12**, wherein the processor is further configured to as part of accessing the database:

access a remote location on the global communication network at an intermediate node thereon;

forward the unique value and unique input device ID to the intermediate node;

wherein the database is disposed at the intermediate node; and

retrieve the associated routing information from the database in the event of a positive match and forward the retrieved routing information back to the first location and connect the first location to the second location in accordance with the retrieved information.

16. The apparatus of claim **12**, wherein the second location represents product information associated with a product.

17. The apparatus of claim **11**, wherein the processor is further configured to:

receive, at the first location, information from the second location in response to connecting the first location to the second location.

18. The apparatus of claim **17**, wherein the processor is further configured to:

present the information received from the second location to a user.

19. The apparatus of claim **18**, wherein the processor as part of the presenting is further adapted to display the information received from the second location via a display at the first location.

20. The apparatus of claim **11** further comprising a browser program configured to perform the connecting the first location to the second location.

* * * * *

Launching a web site using a passive transponder

United States 8,028,036

Issued September 27, 2011

A method of displaying a web page to a user. A triggering device (2502) having a unique code stored therein is provided to the user. The unique code is extracted from the triggering device (2502) with an activation system (302), the activation system (302) disposed on a network (306). Location information associated with the unique code is retrieved from a database (1614 or 310), the location...

Method and apparatus for utilizing an audibly coded signal to conduct commerce over the internet

United States 8,005,985

Issued August 23, 2011

A method and apparatus for utilizing a coded audio/video signal to conduct commerce over the Internet. Broadcast information is broadcast from a remote location on a secondary network containing video over the secondary network to a location thereon proximate the location of the user PC. Unique information is encoded in the broadcast information representative of a location on the primary network...

Software downloading using a television broadcast channel

United States 7,996,552

Issued August 9, 2011

A software distribution architecture having a television broadcast system as its infrastructure. Software from a software repository (1600) is mixed into a television broadcast system and transmitted into one or more selected channels at prescribed dates and times. An at-home subscriber, capable of receiving with a receiver (1608) the one or more select channels, switches to the one or more...

Method and apparatus for connecting a user location to one of a plurality of destination locations on a network

United States 7,979,576

Issued July 12, 2011

A method for interconnecting a user's location to a destination location on a network. The unique information is received at the user's location, which unique information has no associated routing information embedded therein. Network routing information is associated with the received unique information in response to receipt thereof. The user's location is then interconnected to the...

Launching a web site using a passive transponder

United States 7,975,022

Issued July 5, 2011

A method of displaying a web page to a user. A triggering device having a unique code stored therein is provided to the user. The unique code is extracted from the triggering device with an activation system, the activation system disposed on a network. Location information associated with the unique code is retrieved from a database, the location information corresponding to a location of the...

Method and apparatus for completing, securing and conducting an E-commerce transaction

United States 7,930,213
Issued

A method of conducting and on-line transaction. A user at a PC (302) of a first location completes a profile information sheet and transmits it across a secure network (2708) to a central registration server (2704) at a second location also disposed on the network (306). The central registration server (2704) transmits a unique bar code and associated unique ID back to the user PC (302) at the...

Method for connecting a wireless device to a remote location on a network

United States 7,925,780
Issued April 12, 2011

A method for connecting a wireless device to a remote location on a computer network. A beacon signal is transmitted from a beacon unit to a beacon signal receiver circuit disposed with a wireless device. The beacon signal includes components indicative of a first code associated with a remote location and of a second code associated with an attribute of the beacon unit. A first message packet...

Input device for allowing input of unique digital code to a user's computer to control access thereof to a web site

United States 7,912,961
Issued March 22, 2011

A method for controlling a computer is disclosed wherein one or more remote locations disposed on a network are accessed in response to scanning an optical code. A first computer disposed on the network connects to a scanner for scanning the optical code of a product by a user. The scanner is uniquely identified with a scanner distributor by a scanner identification number. A second computer...

Method and apparatus for utilizing a unique transaction code to update a magazine subscription over the internet

United States 7,912,760
Issued March 22, 2011

A method for completing an electronic commerce transaction over a global communication network initiated between a vendor and a potential consumer. The method includes the steps of associating a unique transaction code with the initiated transaction between the vendor and the potential consumer for use by the consumer in completing a specific electronic commerce transaction; associating user...

Automatic configuration of equipment software

United States 7,908,467

Issued

An architecture for automatically configuring software of a piece of equipment. The piece of equipment is in communication with a network, the piece of equipment having one or more machine-resolvable codes associated therewith. The piece of equipment connects to a remote location disposed on the network in response to reading a select one of the one or more machine-resolvable codes with a reader....

Accessing a vendor web site using personal account information retrieved from a credit card company web site

United States 7,904,344

Issued March 8, 2011

A method of accessing a vendor web site (3422) over a global communication packet-switched network (306) using personal account information of a credit card (3400) retrieved from a credit card company server (3300) on the network (306). At a user location disposed on the network, a machine-resolvable code (MRC) (3402) of the credit card (3400) of a user is read with a reading device (3410). Coded...

Method and apparatus for utilizing an audible signal to induce a user to select an E-commerce function

United States 7,900,224

Issued March 1, 2011

A method for delivering advertising to a consumer over a broadcast media/global communication network combination. An advertisement broadcast is generated comprised of a general program and associated advertising dispersed there through for broadcast over a broadcast media which is directed to a general class of consumers. Unique information is embedded in the broadcast for inducing a consumer to...

Method and apparatus for accessing a remote location by receiving a product code

United States 7,886,017

Issued February 8, 2011

A method for controlling a computer is disclosed wherein one or more remote locations disposed on a network are accessed in response to accessing a product code. A first computer

disposed on the network connects to a device for accessing the product code of a product by a user. The device is uniquely identified with a device distributor by a device identification number. A second computer...

Input device having positional and scanning capabilities

United States 7,870,189

Issued January 11, 2011

A multi-purpose input device (2500) for providing conventional positional tracking, and one or more read capabilities for automatically connecting a user PC (302) to remote node. In one embodiment, a user reads optically encoded indicia (1606) of a product by passing the input device (2500) thereover. A software interface (2505) processes the read information, assembles a message packet, and...

Method for interfacing scanned product information with a source for the product over a global network

United States 7,822,829

Issued October 26, 2010

A method for interfacing scanned product information with a source for the product over a global network. A method is provided for obtaining information regarding the source of a product from a remote information source location on a global communication network utilizing a product code associated with the product and unique thereto. The product code associated with the product is scanned with a...

Portable scanner for enabling automatic commerce transactions

United States 7,819,316

Issued October 26, 2010

A method for initiating and completing a commercial transaction is disclosed that allows a user to acquire and own an article of commerce having associated therewith a machine resolvable code (MRC), the MRC having encoded therein information relating to the article of commerce, the user having unique identification information associated with the user. The MRC is first recognized and a...

Retrieving personal account information from a web site by reading a credit card

United States 7,818,423

Issued October 19, 2010

A method of accessing personal account information of a credit card (3400) over a global communication packet-switched network (306). At a user location disposed on the network (306), a machine-resolvable code (MRC) (3402) of the credit card (3400) of a user is read with a reading device (3410). Coded information is extracted from the MRC (3402). Routing information associated with the coded...

Method and apparatus for allowing a broadcast to remotely control a computer

United States 7,792,696

Issued September 6, 2010

The present invention disclosed and claimed herein comprises a system and method for launching an advertisement on a computer having an audio input interface and a display; an audio output acoustically coupled from a broadcast source to the input interface for outputting an audio signal having encoded therein an advertisement; and a program operable on the computer and responsive to the audio...

Launching a web site using a personal device

United States Launching a web site using a personal device

Issued June 15, 2010

A method of displaying a web page to a user. A triggering device (2500) is provided having a unique code associated therewith, the unique code associated with a remote location on a network of the source of the web page. The unique code is transmitted from the triggering device (2500) to an interface system (302), which interface system (302) is disposed on the network (306) at a triggering...

Network routing utilizing a product code

United States 7,694,020

Issued April 6, 2010

A method for utilizing a product code having product information contained therein for interfacing over a network. A representation of the product information is extracted from the product code, which product code is disposed on or in close association with an associated product. In response to this extraction, network routing information is associated with the product code information.

Method and apparatus for automatic configuration of equipment
United States 7,653,446

Issued January 26, 2010

An architecture for automatically configuring equipment. A piece of equipment connected externally to a user PC has one or more machine-resolvable codes (MRCs) associated therewith. The piece of equipment receives configuration information from a remote location disposed on the network in response to reading a select one of the one or more MRCs with a reader. Configuration information associated...

Method and apparatus for matching a user's use profile in commerce with a broadcast
United States 7,636,788

Issued

A method for advertising over a network and broadcast media combination. A user's computer at a location on the network is operable to receive a signal from a broadcast generated by an advertiser, which signal has embedded therein unique coded information. The user's computer is connected to an advertiser's location in response to extracting a representation of the audio signal...

Method and apparatus for utilizing an existing product code to issue a match to a predetermined location on a global network

United States 7,596,786

Issued September 29, 2009

A method for providing an interconnection relationship between a product and a desired location on a global communications network. A machine readable product code is disposed on the product machine readable product code, the machine readable product code having encoded product information contained therein. The product code has no routing information embedded therein which would allow the...

Method for configuring a piece of equipment with the use of an associated machine resolvable code

United States 7,558,838

Issued July 7, 2009

An architecture for automatically configuring equipment interfaced to a computer. A computer which is in communication with a network, is provided having the piece of equipment interfaced to the computer and having associated therewith one or more machine-resolvable codes (MRCs). The computer connects to a remote location disposed on the network in response to a select one of the one or more MRCs...

Software downloading using a television broadcast channel

United States 7,548,988

Issued June 16, 2009

A software distribution architecture having a television broadcast system as its infrastructure. Software from a software repository (1600) is mixed into a television broadcast system and transmitted into one or more selected channels at prescribed dates and times. An at-home subscriber, capable of receiving with a receiver (1608) the one or more select channels, switches to the one or more...

Method and apparatus for opening and launching a web browser in response to an audible signal

United States 7,536,478

Issued May 19, 2009

The present invention disclosed and claimed herein comprises a system and method for launching a web browser on a network comprising a computer having an all new input interface and a communication interface coupled to a computer network; said audio input coupled to the audio output of a source for receiving an audio signal having encoded therein a unique code that is associated with a...

Method and apparatus for accessing a remote location with an optical reader having a programmable memory system

United States 7,533,177

Issued May 12, 2009

A method of accessing a remote location on a network using an optical reader. The optical reader includes an optical scanning system, a programmable memory system and an output circuit and is user-switchable between a scan mode, a record mode and a playback mode. The optical reader transmits a code to a first computer disposed on the network. When the optical reader is in the scan mode, the code...

Method for interconnecting two locations over a network in response to using a tool

United States 7,526,532

Issued April 28, 2009

A method for accessing information over a network. A tool is utilized in conjunction with an operation on a user's processor at a user location on the network. The tool has associated therewith a unique tool ID. In response to utilizing the tool, the user's location is interconnected on the network to a predetermined destination at a remote location on the network, which destination has...

Control of software interface with information input to access window

United States 7,523,161

Issued April 21, 2009

A method is disclosed for controlling the software interface of a user's computing device to display information on a display in proximity to the physical location of the user's computing device. The interface is operable to display to a user on the display at least one access window that is operable to access information about a product, which access window requires the user to input a...

Method and apparatus for utilizing a unique transaction code to update a magazine subscription over the internet

United States 7,505,922

Issued March 17, 2009

The present invention disclosed herein comprises a method for completing an electronic commerce transaction over a global communication network initiated between a vendor and a

potential consumer. The method includes the steps of associating a unique transaction code with the initiated transaction between the vendor and the potential consumer for use by the consumer in completing a specific...

Launching a web site using a portable scanner

United States 7,496,638

Issued February 24, 2009

A method for a user to access information on a network. Information from a machine recognizable code (MRC) (1606) is extracted at a user location, which MRC (1606) has associated therewith routing information to a remote location (312) on the network. The extracted information from the MRC (1606) is wirelessly transmitted to a network interface device (302) in response to the information being...

Controlling a PC using a tone from a cellular telephone

United States 7,493,384

Issued February 17, 2009

A method and apparatus for accessing information over a network (306) from a remote location (312) on the network (306) for delivery to a user PC (302). A cellular telephone (2500) is provided having a functional mode for web access over the network (306). A button (2502) on the phone is associated with the functional mode. The button on the phone (2500) is activated by a user to induce the...

Performing an e-commerce transaction from credit card account information retrieved from a credit card company web site

United States 7,493,283

Issued February 17, 2009

A method of conducting an e-commerce transaction on a global communication network (306) by using personal account information of a credit card retrieved from a credit card company server on the network (306). At a user location disposed on the network, a machine-resolvable code (MRC) (3402) of the credit card (3400) of a user is read with a reading device (3410). Coded information is extracted...

Method and apparatus for allowing a remote site to interact with an intermediate database to facilitate access to the remote site

United States 7,487,259

Issued February 3, 2009

Method and apparatus for allowing a remote site to interact with an intermediate database to facilitate access to the remote site a method for delivering information from a source on a global communication network to destination location thereon. A unique code is associated with an advertising action associated with the source location. The unique code is stored in a database and routing...

Method and apparatus for launching a web browser in response to scanning of product information

United States 7,440,993

Issued October 21, 2008

A method for interconnecting a user's location to a destination location on a network. The unique information is received at the user's location, which unique information has no associated routing information embedded therein. Network routing information is associated with the received unique information in response to receipt thereof. The user's location is then interconnected to the...

Method and apparatus for utilizing an audibly coded signal to conduct commerce over the internet

United States 7,437,475

Issued October 14, 2008

A Method and apparatus for utilizing a coded audio/video signal to conduct commerce over the Internet. Broadcast information is broadcast from a remote location on a secondary network containing video over the secondary network to a location thereon proximate the location of the user PC. Unique information is encoded in the broadcast information representative of a location on the primary network...

Input device for allowing interface to a web site in association with a unique input code

United States 7,428,499

Issued September 23, 2008

An input device for allowing interface to a web site in association with a unique input code. A method for interconnecting a first location on a global communication network with a second location thereon is disclosed. An input device is provided at the first location on the global communication network having associated therewith a unique input device ID. A product code disposed on a product is...

Method using database for facilitating computer based access to a location on a network after scanning a barcode disposed on a product

United States 7,424,521

Issued September 9, 2008

A visual indicia for facilitating computer based access of a network by consumer. A machine readable code is disposed on a surface having encoded therein information as to a product or a surface, which machine readable code has no routing information contained therein to allow a user to access any location on a network. A visual indicia is disposed on the surface indicative of a relationship...

Method for interfacing scanned product information with a source for the product over a global network

United States 7,415,511

Issued August 19, 2008

A method for interfacing scanned product information with a source for the product over a global network. A method is provided for obtaining information regarding the source of a product from a remote information source location on a global communication network utilizing a product code associated with the product and unique thereto. The product code associated with the product is scanned with a...

Method for conducting a contest using a network

United States 7,412,666

Issued August 12, 2008

A method for conducting a contest using a network is provided. A plurality of pick spaces, a virtual display fixture, and a plurality of virtual articles of commerce are displayed on the screen of a user computer. The user computer is disposed at a user site and operably connected to the network. Initially, the virtual articles of commerce are arrayed on the virtual display fixture. At least one...

Method and apparatus for controlling a user's pc through a broadcast communication to archive information in the user's pc

United States 7,398,548

Issued July 8, 2008

A method for allowing a consumer to access an advertiser's location over a global communication network. A normal broadcast program is broadcast to a class of consumers having a unique signal embedded therein, which unique signal embedded therein is associated with a particular advertiser and a predetermined location on the network. Additionally, the unique signal has encoded therein a unique...

Portable scanner for enabling automatic commerce transactions

United States 7,392,945

Issued July 1, 2008

A method for initiating and completing a commercial transaction to acquire an article of commerce (2502). The article of commerce (2502) has associated therewith a machine resolvable code (MRC) (2504). The MRC (2504) has encoded therein information relating to the article of commerce (2502). The encoded information in the MRC (2504) is extracted therefrom and unique identification information...

Method for utilizing visual cue in conjunction with web access

United States 7,392,312

Issued June 24, 2008

The use of a visual indicia or cue facilitates computer based access of a network by a consumer witnessing a presentation. A visual indicia or cue is provided during the presentation indicative of a relationship between the visual indicia or cue in the presence of a location on a network. This allows this location on the network to be accessed by a computer having an appropriate input device for...

Method for conducting a contest using a network

United States 7,392,285

Issued June 24, 2008

A method for conducting a contest using a network is provided. A plurality of pick spaces and a rolling counter are displayed on a screen of a computer operably connected to the network at a user site. The rolling counter constitutes successive ones of a plurality of available characters, each character being displayed for a preselected duration. Each time the user performs a predefined selection...

Launching a web site using a personal device

United States 7,386,600

Issued June 10, 2008

A method of displaying a web page to a user. A triggering device (2500) is provided having a unique code associated therewith, the unique code associated with a remote location on a network of the source of the web page. The unique code is transmitted from the triggering device (2500) to an interface system (302), which interface system (302) is disposed on the network (306) at a triggering...

Method and apparatus for tracking user profile and habits on a global network

United States 7,383,333

Issued June 3, 2008

A method and apparatus for tracking network activity of a user. A user PC (302) disposed on a network (306) runs tracking software which initially requires registration to a registration server (2500). The registration process is initiated by the user entering user information into the tracking software for transmission to the registration server (2500). In response to registration, the...

Method and apparatus for accessing a remote location with a reader having a dedicated memory system

United States 7,383,319

Issued June 3, 2008

A method of accessing a remote location on a network using an optical reader. The optical reader has an optical scanning system and a dedicated address memory system. The optical scanning system, in response to the user scanning an encoded indicia therewith, sends to a first computer disposed on the network a scan code indicative of information encoded in the scanned indicia. The dedicated...

Accessing a vendor web site using personal account information retrieved from a credit card company web site

United States 7,379,901

Issued May 27, 2008

A method of accessing a vendor web site (3422) over a global communication packet-switched network (306) using personal account information of a credit card (3400) retrieved from a credit card company server (3300) on the network (306). At a user location disposed on the network, a machine-resolvable code (MRC) (3402) of the credit card (3400) of a user is read with a reading device (3410). Coded...

Software downloading using a television broadcast channel

United States 7,370,114

Issued May 6, 2008

A software distribution architecture having a television broadcast system as its infrastructure. Software from a software repository (1600) is mixed into a television broadcast system and transmitted into one or more selected channels at prescribed dates and times. An at-home subscriber, capable of receiving with a receiver (1608) the one or more select channels, switches to the one or more...

Presentation of web page content based upon computer video resolution

United States 7,346,694

Issued March 18, 2008

An architecture for customizing the amount of web page banner advertising content presented to a user. When a user accesses a server node (102) disposed on a network (104), the user computer (100) provides video resolution information to the server node (102). The server node (102) transmits a web page to the user node (100) which corresponds to the video resolution information of the user node...

Network routing utilizing a product code

United States 7,321,941

Issued January 22, 2008

A method for utilizing a product code having product information contained therein for interfacing over a network. The product information is extracted from the product code, which product code is disposed on or in close association with an associated product. In response to this extraction, network routing information is associated with the product code information

Method and apparatus for utilizing an audibly coded signal to conduct commerce over the internet

United States 7,318,106

Issued January 8, 2008

A Method and apparatus for utilizing an audibly coded signal to conduct commerce over the Internet. Broadcast information is broadcast from a remote location on a secondary network over the secondary network to a location, thereon proximate the location of the user PC on a primary network. Unique information is encoded in the broadcast information representative of a location on the primary...

Optical reader with ultraviolet wavelength capability

United States 7,314,173

Issued January 1, 2008

An optical reader is provided for reading a bar code having ultraviolet-wavelength-responsive properties. The optical reader includes an ultraviolet light source, a photodetector, an optical system and a decoder. The ultraviolet light source generates ultraviolet light having a wavelength shorter than visible light and longer than X-rays for illuminating a target region. The photodetector...

Method and apparatus for automatic configuration of equipment

United States 7,308,483

Issued December 11, 2007

An architecture for automatically configuring equipment. A piece of equipment connected externally to a user PC has one or more machine-resolvable codes (MRCs) associated therewith. The piece of equipment receives configuration information from a remote location disposed on the network in response to reading a select one of the one or more MRCs with a reader. Configuration information associated...

Aiming indicia for a bar code and method of use

United States 7,296,746

Issued

An aiming indicia is provided for a bar code comprising a sequence of parallel code bars and intervening code spaces disposed along a longitudinal code axis in accordance with a predefined standard. The aiming indicia comprises a non-encoded graphic element disposed on the longitudinal code axis adjacent the bar code and spaced apart from the nearest code bars by a distance of at least 10 times a...

Method and apparatus for opening and launching a web browser in response to an audible signal

United States 7,287,091

Issued October 23, 2007

The present invention disclosed and claimed herein comprises a system and method for launching a web browser on a network comprising a computer having an all new input interface and a communication interface coupled to a computer network; said audio input coupled to the audio output of a source for receiving an audio signal having encoded therein a unique code that is associated with a...

Method and apparatus for matching a user's use profile in commerce with a broadcast

United States 7,284,066

Issued October 16, 2007

A method for advertising over a network and broadcast media combination. A user's computer at a location on the network is operable to receive a signal from a broadcast generated by an advertiser, which signal has embedded therein unique coded information. The user's computer

is connected to an advertiser's location in response to extracting the unique coded information from the audio...

Bar code scanner and software interface interlock for performing encrypted handshaking and for disabling the scanner or input device in case of handshaking operation failure

United States 7,257,619

Issued August 14, 2007

An interlocking architecture for a software interface and a bar code scanner. Upon power-up, a handshaking operation is performed between a scanner (1600) having a scanner processor (2600) and a computer processor (2612) of a computer (302) based upon the code stored in the NV memory (2602) of the scanner (1600) and a unique code associated with the software interface running on the computer...

Digital ID for selecting web browser and use preferences of a user during use of a web application

United States 7,257,614

Issued August 14, 2007

A browser configuration architecture where input of a unique user ID automatically configures those browser applications preselected for auto-configuration from entries of a user preferences sheet. The user preferences sheet (2500) is part of the browser control software (2502) used for storing user preferences associated with one or more browser applications (2506, 2508, and 2510) loaded on a...

Optical reader and use

United States 7,240,840

Issued July 10, 2007

An optical reader is provided for reading a symbol representing information having areas of different light reflectivity. The optical reader comprises a radiant energy source, a photodetector, an optical system and a decoder. The radiant energy source generates a radiant energy for illuminating a target region. The photodetector generates output electrical signals indicative of the radiant energy...

Automatic configuration of equipment software

United States 7,237,104

Issued June 26, 2007

An architecture for automatically configuring software of a piece of equipment. The piece of equipment is in communication with a network, the piece of equipment having one or more machine-resolvable codes associated therewith. The piece of equipment connects to a remote location disposed on the network in response to reading a select one of the one or more machine-resolvable codes with a reader....

Method and apparatus for directing an existing product code to a remote location

United States 7,228,282

Issued June 5, 2007

A method for interfacing a user location on a network to a destination location on the network is disclosed. A bar code having product information contained therein relating to an associated product is first scanned with a scanner, which bar code has no network routing information contained therein. The product information contained within the bar code is then extracted. Routing information over...

Method and apparatus for accessing a remote location with an optical reader having a dedicated memory system

United States 7,197,543

Issued March 27, 2007

A method of accessing a remote location on a network using an optical reader. The optical reader has an optical scanning system and a dedicated address memory system. The optical scanning system, in response to the user scanning an encoded indicia therewith, sends to a first computer disposed on the network a scan code indicative of information encoded in the scanned indicia. The dedicated...

Method for connecting a wireless device to a remote location on a network

United States 7,191,247

Issued March 13, 2007

A method for connecting a wireless device to a remote location on a computer network. A beacon signal is transmitted from a beacon unit disposed at a first geographic location. The beacon signal includes components indicative of a first code and of a second code, the first code being associated with a remote location on a computer network and the second code being associated with an attribute of...

Method and apparatus for utilizing an existing product code to issue a match to a predetermined location on a global network

United States 7,159,037

Issued January 2, 2007

A method for providing an interconnection relationship between a product and a desired location on a global communications network. A machine readable product code is disposed on the product machine readable product code, the machine readable product code having encoded product information contained therein. The product code has no routing information embedded therein which would allow the...

Method and apparatus for launching a web site with non-standard control input device

United States 7,117,240

Issued October 3, 2006

A method for launching a web browser application on a user's computer. A browser application is provided on the user's computer that is launchable in response to predetermined browser inputs being received by the user's computer. A non-browser input is provided that is not a

portion of the set of predetermined browser inputs. This non-browser is correlated to the input to simulate one...

Battery pack having integral optical reader for wireless communication device

United States 7,089,291

Issued August 8, 2006

A battery pack for a wireless communication device comprises a housing, at least one battery disposed within the housing and an optical reader disposed within the housing. The housing is adapted to be removably attachable to a wireless communication device. The housing includes an external shell defining an optical port there through and has an operational power interface and a data interface...

Method and apparatus for controlling a user's PC through an audio-visual broadcast to archive information in the user's PC

United States 7,069,582

Issued June 27, 2006

A method for allowing a consumer to access an advertiser's location over a global communication network. A normal broadcast program is broadcast to a class of consumers having a unique signal embedded therein, which unique signal embedded therein is associated with a particular advertiser and a predetermined location on the network. Additionally, the unique signal has encoded therein a unique...

Method for controlling a computer using an embedded unique code in the content of CD media

United States 7,043,536

Issued April 9, 2006

A method for allowing a user PC (1702) to be controlled in order to effect a connection between the user PC (1702) and a destination node (1706) on a network (306). This is facilitated through an audio source (1700) wherein compact disk recording media has embedded therein an audio signal. When the compact disk recording media is played, the audio signal is extracted by an audio extractor (1600)...

Method of controlling a computer using an embedded unique code in the content of DVD media

United States 7,010,577

Issued March 7, 2006

A method for allowing a user PC to be controlled in order to effect a connection between the user PC and a destination node on a network. This is facilitated through an audio source wherein the content of digital video disk recording media has embedded therein an audio signal. When the recording media is played, the audio signal is extracted by an audio extractor and transmitted to the user PC,...

Method and apparatus for allowing a remote site to interact with an intermediate database to facilitate access to the remote site

United States 6,985,962

Issued January 10, 2006

Method and apparatus for allowing a remote site to interact with an intermediate database to facilitate access to the remote site a method for delivering information from a source on a global communication network to a second and a user location thereon. A unique code is associated with an advertising action associated with the source location. The unique code is stored in a database and routing...

Input device for allowing input of a unique digital code to a user's computer to control access thereof to a web site

United States 6,985,954

Issued January 10, 2006

An input device for allowing input of a unique digital code to a user's computer to control access thereof to a web site. A method for connecting a user computer at a first location on a network with a second location on the network through use of a coded symbol having contained therein encoded information associated with routing information on the network to the second location thereover is...

Audible designation for a node on a communication network

United States 6,981,059

Issued December 27, 2005

An audible designation for a node on a communication network A method is provided for allowing any of a plurality of first locations on a global communication network to access a specific and determinable second location on the global communication network. A unique audio signature is defined for the specific and determinable second location on the global communication network, which unique audio...

Method and apparatus for delivering information from a remote site on a network based on statistical information

United States 6,973,438

Issued December 6, 2006

A method and apparatus are disclosed for delivering information, from a content location on a global communication network (GCN) dynamically selected according to statistical information, to a user location thereon. In a computer database, GCN routing information for each of a plurality of content locations on the GCN are associated with a predefined combination of one of a plurality of...

Method for conducting a contest using a network

United States 6,970,916

Issued November 29, 2005

A method for conducting a contest using a network is provided. Displayed, on a practical screen of a user computer operably connected to the network at a user site, is a plurality of pick spaces, a virtual television set including a first virtual screen, and a virtual computer including a second virtual screen. The apparent area of the first virtual screen constitutes a first display area of the...

Method and apparatus for embedding routing information to a remote web site in an audio/video track

United States 6,970,914
Issued November 29, 2005

A redirect system is provided which is operable to redirect information over a network 1610. This information is associated with a compressed MP3 audio file which is initially transmitted through the network from a source 1612 to a user PC 1600. The user PC 1600 will then play the information and, upon playing the information, embedded information within the audio file will be detected by an...

System and apparatus for connecting a wireless device to a remote location on a network

United States 6,961,555
Issued November 1, 2005

A system for connecting a wireless device to a remote location on a computer network. The wireless device (2510) includes a processor (2714) and a transmitter/receiver (2716) for sending and receiving radio frequency signals (2516) to provide two-way digital communication between the processor and the computer network (306). The system comprises a beacon unit (2502) and a beacon signal receiver...

Launching a web site using a portable scanner

United States 6,877,032
Issued April 5, 2005

A method for a user to access information on a network. Information from a machine recognizable code (MRC) (1606) is extracted at a user location, which MRC (1606) has associated therewith routing information to a remote location (312) on the network. The extracted information from the MRC (1606) is wirelessly transmitted to a network interface device (302) in response to the information being...

Input device having positional and scanning capabilities

United States 6,868,433
Issued March 15, 2005

A multi-purpose input device (2500) for providing conventional positional tracking, and one or more read capabilities for automatically connecting a user PC (302) to remote node. In one embodiment, a user reads optically encoded indicia (1606) of a product by passing the input device (2500) thereover. A software interface (2505) processes the read information, assembles a message packet, and...

Optical reader and use

United States 6,860,424

Issued March 1, 2005

An optical reader is provided for reading a symbol representing information having areas of different light reflectivity. The optical reader comprises a radiant energy source, a photodetector, an optical system and a decoder. The radiant energy source generates a radiant energy for illuminating a target region. The photodetector generates output electrical signals indicative of the radiant energy...

Web site access manual of a character string into a software interface

United States 6,845,388

Issued January 18, 2005

An architecture for accessing a network server using one or more characters. A user computer (302) disposed on a global communication packet-switched network (306) is operable to communicate with an ARS (308) and a destination server (312) also disclosed on the GCN (306). The user computer (302) runs a software interface which displays a window (2500) to the user via a display (1612). The window...

Aiming indicia for a bar code and method of use

United States 6,843,417

Issued January 18, 2005

An aiming indicia is provided for a bar code comprising a sequence of parallel code bars and intervening code spaces disposed along a longitudinal code axis in accordance with a predefined standard. The aiming indicia comprises a non-encoded graphic element disposed on the longitudinal code axis adjacent the bar code and spaced apart from the nearest code bars by a distance of at least 10 times a...

Method and apparatus for tracking user profile and habits on a global network

United States 6,836,799

Issued December 28, 2004

A method and apparatus for tracking network activity of a user. A user PC (302) disposed on a network (306) runs tracking software which initially requires registration to a registration server (2500). The registration process is initiated by the user entering user information into the tracking software for transmission to the registration server (2500). In response to registration, the...

Method and apparatus for opening and launching a web browser in response to an audible signal

United States 6,829,650

Issued December 7, 2004

The present invention disclosed and claimed herein comprises a system and method for launching a web browser on a network comprising a computer having an all new input interface and a communication interface coupled to a computer network; said audio input coupled to the

audio output of a source for receiving an audio signal having encoded therein a unique code that is associated with a...

Presentation of web page content based upon computer video resolutions

United States 6,829,646

Issued December 7, 2004

An architecture for customizing the amount of web page banner advertising content presented to a user. When a user accesses a server node (102) disposed on a network (104), the user computer (100) provides video resolution information to the server node (102). The server node (102) transmits a web page to the user node (100) which corresponds to the video resolution information of the user node...

Digital ID for selecting web browser and use preferences of a user during use of a web application

United States 6,826,592

Issued November 30, 2004

A browser configuration architecture where input of a unique user ID automatically configures those browser applications preselected for auto-configuration from entries of a user preferences sheet. The user preferences sheet (2500) is part of the browser control software (2502) used for storing user preferences associated with one or more browser applications (2506, 2508, and 2510) loaded on a...

Method and apparatus for accessing a remote location with an optical reader having a programmable memory system

United States 6,823,388

Issued November 23, 2004

A method of accessing a remote location on a network using an optical reader. The optical reader includes an optical scanning system, a programmable memory system and an output circuit and is user-switchable between a scan mode, a record mode and a playback mode. The optical reader transmits a code to a first computer disposed on the network. When the optical reader is in the scan mode, the code...

Method for interfacing scanned product information with a source for the product over a global network

United States 6,816,894

Issued November 9, 2004

A method for interfacing scanned product information with a source for the product over a global network. A method is provided for obtaining information regarding the source of a product from a remote information source location on a global communication network utilizing a product code associated with the product and unique thereto. The product code associated with the product is scanned with a...

Method for configuring a piece of equipment with the use of an associated machine resolvable code

United States 6,792,452

Issued September 14, 2004

An architecture for automatically configuring equipment interfaced to a computer. A computer which is in communication with a network, is provided having the piece of equipment interfaced to the computer and having associated therewith one or more machine-resolvable codes (MRCs). The computer connects to a remote location disposed on the network in response to a select one of the one or more MRCs...

Method for conducting a contest using a network

United States 6,791,588

Issued September 14, 2004

A method for conducting a contest using a network is provided. A plurality of pick spaces, a virtual display fixture, and a plurality of virtual articles of commerce are displayed on the screen of a user computer. The user computer is disposed at a user site and operably connected to the network. Initially, the virtual articles of commerce are arrayed on the virtual display fixture. At least one...

Optical reader with ultraviolet wavelength capability

United States 6,758,398

Issued July 6, 2004

An optical reader is provided for reading a bar code having ultraviolet-wavelength-responsive properties. The optical reader includes an ultraviolet light source, a photodetector, an optical system and a decoder. The ultraviolet light source generates ultraviolet light having a wavelength shorter than visible light and longer than X-rays for illuminating a target region. The photodetector...

Bar code scanner and software interface interlock for performing encrypted handshaking and for disabling the scanner in case of handshaking operation failure

United States 6,757,715

Issued June 29, 2004

An interlocking architecture for a software interface and a bar code scanner. Upon power-up, a handshaking operation is performed between a scanner (1600) having a scanner processor (2600) and a computer processor (2612) of a computer (302) based upon the code stored in the NV memory (2602) of the scanner (1600) and a unique code associated with the software interface running on the computer...

Method and apparatus for accessing a remote location with an optical reader having a dedicated memory system

United States 6,754,698

Issued June 22, 2004

A method of accessing a remote location on a network using an optical reader. The optical reader has an optical scanning system and a dedicated address memory system. The optical scanning system, in response to the user scanning an encoded indicia therewith, sends to a first computer disposed on the network a scan code indicative of information encoded in the scanned indicia. The dedicated...

Method and apparatus for accessing a remote location by scanning an optical code

United States 6,745,234

Issued June 1, 2004

A method for controlling a computer is disclosed wherein one or more remote locations disposed on a network are accessed in response to scanning an optical code. A first computer disposed on the network connects to a scanner for scanning the optical code of a product by a user. The scanner is uniquely identified with a scanner distributor by a scanner identification number. A second computer...

Method and apparatus for configuring configurable equipment with configuration information received from a remote location

United States 6,725,260

Issued April 20, 2004

An architecture for automatically configuring equipment. A piece of equipment connected externally to a user PC has one or more machine-resolvable codes (MRCs) associated therewith. The piece of equipment receives configuration information from a remote location disposed on the network in response to reading a select one of the one or more MRCs with a reader. Configuration information associated...

Unique bar code for indicating a link between a product and a remote location on a web network

United States 6,708,208

Issued March 16, 2004

A unique bar code for indicating a link between a product and a remote location on a web network. The present invention dicsclosed and claimed herein, in one aspect thereof, comprises system for connecting between a first location at a user's site on a network and a second and remote location on a network. A unique ornamental symbol encoded with a plurality of dark and light areas is provided...

Automatic configuration of equipment software

United States 6,704,864

Issued March 9, 2004

An architecture for automatically configuring software of a piece of equipment. The piece of equipment is in communication with a network, the piece of equipment having one or more machine-resolvable codes associated therewith. The piece of equipment connects to a remote location disposed on the network in response to reading a select one of the one or more machine-resolvable codes with a reader....

Method and apparatus for accessing a remote location by sensing a machine-resolvable code

United States 6,701,369

Issued March 2, 2004

A method for controlling a computer wherein one or more remote locations disposed on a network are accessed in response to sensing a machine-resolvable code. A computer disposed on a network is operably connected to an input device for sensing a machine-resolvable code. A software application which includes a software identification code runs on the computer. In response to sensing a...

Method for interconnecting two locations over a network in response to using a tool

United States 6,701,354

Issued March 2, 2004

A method for accessing information over a network. A tool is utilized in conjunction with an operation on a user's processor at a user location on the network. The tool has associated therewith a unique tool ID. In response to utilizing the tool, the user's location is interconnected on the network to a predetermined destination at a remote location on the network, which destination has...

Method and apparatus for controlling a user's pc through an audio-visual broadcast to archive information in the users pc

United States 6,697,949

Issued February 24, 2004

A method for allowing a consumer to access an advertiser's location over a global communication network. A normal broadcast program is broadcast to a class of consumers having a unique signal embedded therein, which unique signal embedded therein is associated with a particular advertiser and a predetermined location on the network. Additionally, the unique signal has encoded therein a unique...

(PT) Método para conectar por meio de interface uma informação escaneada de produto a uma fonte do produto através de uma rede global

Mexico PI9913624

Issued January 15, 2002

(PT) "MéTODO PARA CONECTAR POR MEIO DE INTERFACE UMA INFORMAçãO ESCANEADA DE PRODUTO A UMA FONTE DO PRODUTO ATRAVéS DE UMA REDE GLOBAL". Método para conectar por meio de interface uma informação escaneada de produto com o fabricante do produto através de uma rede global de comunicação (306). Após escanear a informação de...

PI9913623 -Método para controlar um computador com um sinal de áudio

Europe PI9913623

Issued January 15, 2002

"MéTODO PARA CONTROLAR UM COMPUTADOR COM UM SINAL DE áUDIO". Método para controlar um computador (302) ao se inserir um sinal analógico (111) no computador (302)

para controlar um aplicativo de software navegador de rede. O sinal analógico (111) contém um sinal de acionamento que ativa um software de proprietário, e um identificador de produto. O...

Remote control having an optical indicia reader

United States 6,694,356

Issued February 17, 2004

A method for a user to access information on a network (306). A remote control device (3700) is provided operating in a first and control mode with internally generated control commands and in a second and scanning mode. In the control mode, an appliance at a user location is controlled by wirelessly transmitting the control commands to the appliance. In the scanning mode, a machine recognizable...

Unique bar code

United States 6,688,522

Issued February 10, 2004

A bar code for encoding information in machine-readable form is provided. The bar code comprises a character string including a plurality of characters disposed side-by-side along a longitudinal code axis. Each character is formed by a sequence of code bars and intervening code spaces, the code bars being parallel to one another and to a line defining a bar axis which intersects the code axis....

Method for controlling a computer using an embedded unique code in the content of video tape media

United States 6,643,692

Issued November 4, 2003

A method for allowing a user PC (1702) to be controlled in order to effect a connection between the user PC (1702) and a destination node (1706) on a network (306). This is facilitated through an audio source (1700) wherein the content of a video tape recording media has embedded therein an audio signal. When the video tape media is played, the audio signal is extracted by an audio extractor...

Method and apparatus for utilizing an audibly coded signal to conduct commerce over the internet

United States 6,636,896

Issued October 21, 2003

A method and apparatus for utilizing a coded audio/video signal to conduct commerce over the Internet. Broadcast information is broadcast from a remote location on a secondary network containing video over the secondary network to a location thereon proximate the location of the user PC. Unique information is encoded in the broadcast information representative of a location on the primary network...

Method for conducting a contest using a network

United States 6,636,892

Issued October 21, 2003

A method for conducting a contest using a network is provided. A plurality of pick spaces and a rolling counter are displayed on a screen of a computer operably connected to the network at a user site. The rolling counter constitutes successive ones of a plurality of available characters, each character being displayed for a preselected duration. Each time the user performs a predefined selection...

Method and system for conducting a contest using a network

United States 6,631,404

Issued October 7, 2003

A method for conducting a contest using a network. A selected article of commerce is identified to a plurality of users remotely disposed at user locations on the network which bears an indicia encoding an identification code which corresponds to the selected article in accordance with an extrinsic standard. An unvalidated entry message packet is then received at a reference location which was...

Interactive Doll

United States 6,629,133

Issued September 30, 2003

An interactive doll is disclosed having one or more sensors contained therein. The one or more sensors are operable to trigger output of a signal from the doll in response to the one or more sensors being activated by physical stimuli of a user. A processor located with the user and the doll at a first node of a global communication network processes the signal. The processor is operable to link...

Method and apparatus for allowing a remote site to interact with an intermediate database to facilitate access to the remote site

United States 6,622,165

Issued September 16, 2003

Method and apparatus for allowing a remote site to interact with an intermediate database to facilitate access to the remote site a method for delivering information from a source on a global communication network to a second and a user location thereon. A unique code is associated with an advertising action associated with the source location. The unique code is stored in a database and routing...

Method for controlling a computer using an embedded unique code in the content of dat media

United States 6,615,268

Issued September 2, 2003

A method for allowing a user PC to be controlled in order to effect a connection between the user PC and a destination node on a network. This is facilitated through an audio source wherein a digital audio tape recording media having embedded therein an audio signal therein.

When the recording media is played, the audio signal is extracted by an audio extractor and transmitted to the user PC, and...

Method and apparatus for utilizing an audibly coded signal to conduct commerce over the internet

United States 6,594,705
Issued July 15, 2003

A Method and apparatus for utilizing an audibly coded signal to conduct commerce over the Internet. Broadcast information is broadcast from a remote location on a secondary network over the secondary network to a location thereon proximate the location of the user PC on a primary network. Unique information is encoded in the broadcast information representative of a location on the primary...

Method and apparatus for controlling a computer from a remote location

United States 6,526,449
Issued February 25, 2003

A method for controlling a user computer is disclosed wherein a broadcast program is operable to transmit a broadcast to the user in the form of an audio/visual program, in addition to an encoded tone. This encoded tone is detected by the user computer and this information then transmitted to an intermediate node, an ARS (308). This tone is compared in a relational database (1704) to determine is...

Method and system for data transmission from an optical reader

United States 6,384,744
Issued May 7, 2002

A method is provided for transmitting data from an optical reader following scanning by the optical reader of an indica encoding information in accordance with one of a plurality of information encoding types. The method includes determining that a particular one of the plurality of encoding types was used for encoding the scanned indicia. A message packet is then transmitted from the optical...

Routing string indicative of a location of a database on a web associated with a product in commerce

United States 6,377,986
Issued April 23, 2002

A method for controlling a computer is disclosed wherein one or more remote locations disposed on a network are accessed in response to scanning an optical code. A first computer disposed on the network connects to a scanner for scanning the optical code of a product by a user. The scanner is uniquely identified with a scanner distributor by a scanner identification number. A second computer...

Keystroke Automator
United States D432,539

Issued October 24, 2000

The ornamental design for keystroke automator, as shown and described.

Method for controlling a computer with an audio signal

United States 6,098,106

Issued August 1, 2000

A method for controlling a computer by inputting an analog signal into the computer to control a web browser software application. The analog signal contains a trigger signal which activates proprietary software, and a product identifier. The proprietary software launches the web browser application on the computer, extracts the product identifier, and creates an appended data string by appending...

Method of product promotion

United States 6,928,413

Issued August 9, 2005

A method of promoting a product. A user at a user location (100) is induced to obtain a first product having a unique ID from a first vendor to win a prize. The user registers the product via a user computer (102) connected on-line to a central registration server (108) across a packet-switched network (104) by completing a user profile and transmitting the user profile and unique ID to a central...

Método para conectar por meio de interface uma informação escaneada de produto a uma fonte do produto através de uma rede global

Brazil PI9913624

Issued January 15, 2002

(PT) "MéTODO PARA CONECTAR POR MEIO DE INTERFACE UMA INFORMAçãO ESCANEADA DE PRODUTO A UMA FONTE DO PRODUTO ATRAVéS DE UMA REDE GLOBAL". Método para conectar por meio de interface uma informação escaneada de produto com o fabricante do produto através de uma rede global de comunicação (306). Após escanear a informação de...

Método para controlar um computador com um sinal de áudio

Brazil PI9913623

Issued January 15, 2002

"MéTODO PARA CONTROLAR UM COMPUTADOR COM UM SINAL DE áUDIO". Método para controlar um computador (302) ao se inserir um sinal analógico (111) no computador (302) para controlar um aplicativo de software navegador de rede. O sinal analógico (111) contém um sinal de acionamento que ativa um software de proprietário, e um identificador de produto. O...

INDICE DE POINTAGE DESTINE A UN CODE BARRES ET PROCEDE D'UTILISATION

France PCT/US2001/015970

Issued June 12, 2001

(FR)L'invention concerne un indice de pointage destiné à un code barres (4000), comportant une séquence de codes barres parallèles (4012) et d'espaces de code (4014) intercalés disposés le long d'un axe de code longitudinal (4010) selon un standard prédéfini. Ledit indice (4050) de pointage comporte un élément graphique (4052) non...

LECTEUR OPTIQUE ET UTILISATION CORRESPONDANTE
France WO/2001/093184
Issued December 6, 2001

L'invention concerne un lecteur optique permettant de lire un symbole qui représente une information dotée de zones de réflectivité de lumière différente. Le lecteur optique comporte une source d'énergie radiante, un photodétecteur, un système optique et un décodeur. Ladite source génère une énergie radiante permettant...

CODE BARRES UNIQUE
France WO/2001/093187
Issued December 6, 2001

L'invention concerne un code barres destiné à coder des informations sous forme lisible par machine. Ce code barres comporte une chaîne de caractères contenant une pluralité de caractères disposés l'un à côté de l'autre le long d'un axe de code longitudinal. Chaque caractère est formé par une séquence de codes barres...

Input device for allowing interface to a web site in association with a unique input code
United States 8,069,098
Issued November 29, 2011

An input device for allowing interface to a web site in association with a unique input code. A method for interconnecting a first location on a global communication network with a second location thereon is disclosed. An input device is provided at the first location on the global communication network having associated therewith a unique input device ID. A product code disposed on a product is...

(FR) INDICE DE POINTAGE DESTINE A UN CODE BARRES ET PROCEDE D'UTILISATION
Europe WO/2001/093190
Issued

(FR)L'invention concerne un indice de pointage destiné à un code barres (4000), comportant une séquence de codes barres parallèles (4012) et d'espaces de code (4014) intercalés disposés le long d'un axe de code longitudinal (4010) selon un standard prédéfini. Ledit indice (4050) de pointage comporte un élément graphique (4052) non...

(FR) INDICE DE POINTAGE DESTINE A UN CODE BARRES ET PROCEDE D'UTILISATION
Europe WO/2001/093190
Issued June 12, 2001

FR)L'invention concerne un indice de pointage destiné à un code barres (4000), comportant une séquence de codes barres parallèles (4012) et d'espaces de code (4014) intercalés disposés le

long d'un axe de code longitudinal (4010) selon un standard prédéfini. Ledit indice (4050) de pointage comporte un élément graphique (4052) non...

Method and apparatus for accessing a remote location by sensing a machine-resolvable code

United States 8,484,362

Issued July 9, 2013

A method for controlling a computer wherein one or more remote locations disposed on a network are accessed in response to sensing a machine-resolvable code. A computer disposed on a network is operably connected to an input device for sensing a machine-resolvable code. A software application which includes a software identification code runs on the computer. In response to sensing a...

2 inventors:

- **Hutton (Jovan) Pulitzer**
  Founder FevrTech.org, Flip.Ventures, Xplrr.org and Publisher at InvestigatingHistory.org

- **J Jovan Philyaw**

Method and apparatus for accessing a remote location with an optical reader having a programmable memory system

United States 8,296,440

Issued October 23, 2012

An optical reader for accessing a remote location on a network includes an optical scanning system, a memory system, an output circuit for interfacing to a first computer disposed on the network, and a switching device for switching between a scan mode, a record mode and a playback mode. The optical reader further includes a transmitter for transmitting code information representative of a code...

3 inventors:

- **Hutton (Jovan) Pulitzer**
  Founder FevrTech.org, Flip.Ventures, Xplrr.org and Publisher at InvestigatingHistory.org

- **j hutton pulitzer**

- **Doug Davis**
  EVP Technology at West Corporation

Input device for allowing interface to a web site in association with a unique input code

United States 8,069,098

Issued November 29, 2011

An input device for allowing interface to a web site in association with a unique input code. A method for interconnecting a first location on a global communication network with a second location thereon is disclosed. An input device is provided at the first location on the global communication network having associated therewith a unique input device ID. A product code disposed on a product is...

2 inventors:

- **Hutton (Jovan) Pulitzer**
  Founder FevrTech.org, Flip.Ventures, Xplrr.org and Publisher at InvestigatingHistory.org

- **J Jovan Philyaw**

Method and apparatus for accessing a remote location by sensing a machine-resolvable code

United States 8,484,362

Issued July 9, 2013

A method for controlling a computer wherein one or more remote locations disposed on a network are accessed in response to sensing a machine-resolvable code. A computer disposed on a network is operably connected to an input device for sensing a machine-resolvable code. A software application which includes a software identification code runs on the computer. In response to sensing a...

Method and apparatus for accessing a remote location with an optical reader having a programmable memory system

United States 8,296,440

Issued September 23, 2012

An optical reader for accessing a remote location on a network includes an optical scanning system, a memory system, an output circuit for interfacing to a first computer disposed on the network, and a switching device for switching between a scan mode, a record mode and a playback mode. The optical reader further includes a transmitter for transmitting code information representative of a code...

(EN) AUTOMATIC CONFIGURATION OF EQUIPMENT AND SOFTWARE (FR) CONFIGURATION AUTOMATIQUE D'EQUIPEMENT ET DE LOGICIEL

Europe WO/2001/086435

Issued October 5, 2001

(EN)An architecture for automatically configuring equipment. A piece of equipment connected externally to a user PC has one or more machine-resolvable codes (MRCs) associated therewith.

The piece of equipment receives configuration information from a remote location disposed on the network in response to reading a select one of the one or more MRCs with a reader. Configuration information...

Method and apparatus for accessing a remote location by sensing a machine-resolvable code

United States 8,484,362

Issued July 9, 2013

A method for controlling a computer wherein one or more remote locations disposed on a network are accessed in response to sensing a machine-resolvable code. A computer disposed on a network is operably connected to an input device for sensing a machine-resolvable code. A software application which includes a software identification code runs on the computer. In response to sensing a...

2 inventors:

- **Hutton (Jovan) Pulitzer**
  Founder FevrTech.org, Flip.Ventures, Xplrr.org and Publisher at InvestigatingHistory.org

- **jeffry jovan philyaw**

Method for controlling a computer using an embedded unique code in the content of recorded media

United States 8,655,972

Issued February 18, 2014

A method for controlling a computer with recorded information of a recorded media includes embedding a unique code, which unique code does not contain routing information, in recorded information of the recorded media. The unique code is in close association with vendor information, such that the unique code will be output during normal playback of the information on the recorded media. The...

2 inventors:

- **Hutton (Jovan) Pulitzer**
  Founder FevrTech.org, Flip.Ventures, Xplrr.org and Publisher at InvestigatingHistory.org

- **jeffry jovan philyaw**

Method and apparatus for linking a web browser link to a promotional offer

United States 8,712,835

Issued April 29, 2014

A method for offering a promotion to a user. A stimulus is received from a broadcast directed to a user location, the stimulus having unique coded information encoded therein. The unique coded information is extracted from the stimulus by decoding this information. From the decoded information, there is determined routing information for routing over a network to a promotion location on the...

2 inventors:

-
  Hutton (Jovan) Pulitzer
  Founder FevrTech.org, Flip.Ventures, Xplrr.org and Publisher at InvestigatingHistory.org

- **jeffry jovan philyaw**

Method and apparatus for accessing a remote location with an optical reader having a programmable memory system

United States 8,296,440

Issued October 23, 2012

An optical reader for accessing a remote location on a network includes an optical scanning system, a memory system, an output circuit for interfacing to a first computer disposed on the network, and a switching device for switching between a scan mode, a record mode and a playback mode. The optical reader further includes a transmitter for transmitting code information representative of a code...

2 inventors:

-
  Hutton (Jovan) Pulitzer
  Founder FevrTech.org, Flip.Ventures, Xplrr.org and Publisher at InvestigatingHistory.org

- **Jeffry Jovan Philyaw**

Method and apparatus for accessing a remote location by sensing a machine-resolvable code

United States 8,484,362

Issued July 9, 2013

A method for controlling a computer wherein one or more remote locations disposed on a network are accessed in response to sensing a machine-resolvable code. A computer disposed on a network is operably connected to an input device for sensing a machine-resolvable code. A software application which includes a software identification code runs on the computer. In response to sensing a...